Copyright © 2024 Matthew Hagaman

The right of Matthew Hagaman to be identified as the author of this work has been asserted in accordance with the Copyright, Designs, and Patents Act of 1988.

ISBN-13: 979-8364781536

This text is meant to be instructional, and no portion should be considered legal advice.

The accuracy of exact figures may vary from real-world values.

For the most accurate, current, and relevant advice on operating a business, always seek help from an accredited legal or financial expert.

E-Commerce
Innovations, Economics, and the Internet

Matthew Hagaman

A Companion to Illinois State University's TEC 378

Table of Contents

Introduction   1
1.1   A Common Vocabulary   3
      Value and Supply Chains
1.2   A Brief History of E-Commerce   5
      The First Wave
      The Second Wave
      The Third Wave
1.3   A Legal History of E-Commerce   9
      Legislative Actions
      Executive Actions
      Judicial Actions
1.4   The State of E-Commerce Today   19
      Machine Learning
      The Fourth Wave
CS1   Building & Bending E-Commerce   25

Initial Business Tasks   31
2.1   An Overview of Business Models   33
      Legal Structures
2.2   Choosing a Revenue Model   37
      Hybrid Revenue Models
2.3   Identifying Target Markets   41
      Market Segmentation
2.4   Crafting a Corporate Message   45
      Mission and Vision Statements
2.5   Conducting Market Research   47
      Brands and Competitive Advantage
CS2   Products Plus Programs   53

Finding Stakeholders   57
3.1   Talking to Investors   59
      Elevator Pitches
      1-Page Proposals
      Business Plans

3.2	Pre- and Post-Investor Analyses Defining Goals and Objectives SWOT Analyses	67
3.3	Hiring Talent The Gig Economy	73
3.4	Stakeholder Privacy Physical Considerations Technical Considerations Sociological Considerations	79
CS3	Concerning Sharks	83

Building a Web Site — **87**

4.1	Web Infrastructure The Path of a Packet Disrupting Web Infrastructure	89
4.2	Web Hosts Web Server Classifications Other Hosting Considerations	95
4.3	Web Navigation	101
4.4	Web Design Creating Wireframes Creating Mockups Creating Prototypes	103
4.5	Web Development Web Server Software Stacks Developing for Accessibility Resources for Language Learning Libraries and Frameworks	111
4.6	Web Analytics Analytics in Product Testing	123
CS4	Industrial Analytics	127

Communicating with Stakeholders — **131**
5.1 Marketing Strategies — 133
    Product Strategies
    Place Strategies
    Promotion Strategies
    Pricing Strategies
    Revisiting Objectives
5.2 Advertising Strategies — 139
    Customer Acquisition and Retention
    Practical Advertising Advice
5.3 Social Media — 145
    Returns from Social Media Engagement
5.4 Customer Relationship Management — 149
    Stages of the Customer Life Cycle
5.5 Marketing Plans — 153
CS5 Viral Marketing — 157

Business Finances — **161**
6.1 Start-Up Expenses — 163
    Fixed Assets
    Operating Capital
    Sources of Funding
6.2 Payroll — 167
6.3 Sales Forecasts — 169
6.4 Operating Expenses — 173
6.5 Financial Analyses — 175

References — 177

Index of Abbreviations — 199

Chapter 1.0 **Introduction**

Virtually everyone on Earth is affected by the Internet, even if they don't have direct access. The Internet has a role to play in nearly every societal task, but especially those tasks related to economic activity and commerce.

E-commerce is a term used to describe any transaction that happens electronically. We often use e-commerce to describe typical commerce (buying and selling), but there are many transactions that may not involve buying or selling. For example, e-commerce frequently describes the transfer of information. As most top companies will tell you, information has value. (It is no coincidence that four of the top five companies in the world made their fortune with information: Apple, Microsoft, Alphabet, and Amazon.com all link information in the cloud with personal information and personal devices. The fifth, Nvidia, makes hardware to process that information!)

As we explore the broad topic of e-commerce, we will also explore innovation and entrepreneurship. Together, we will learn how the world wide web enables us to set up a financially sound business. The core of this process is keeping stakeholders in mind: we must be able to identify, serve, and stay in touch with customers as well as investors, employees, suppliers, and others.

In any industry, entire volumes could be written to describe specialized vocabulary. This is especially true in e-commerce, where industries collide.

Section 1.1 A Common Vocabulary

E-commerce exists at the intersection of every other industry. Many roles related to e-commerce require communicating with different stakeholders; to be successful, we must understand the vocabulary and abbreviations used by each group. Those of us entering the world of e-commerce must understand the languages of business, economics, and information technology as well as the vocabulary used at every stage in designing, producing, and supporting goods and services.

We already defined e-commerce in the introduction to this text, but we should also define a number of other terms and abbreviations we will encounter throughout the book.

In most cases, we will use the word product to describe both goods and services because the processes we follow and the decisions we make are often identical.

Business is all about serving stakeholders, from customers and employees to investors and suppliers. Anyone who can be affected by a business decision can be considered a stakeholder. As an example, raising the price of your product affects every stakeholder. Customers will need to pay more, which may reduce how much they can buy. As customer demand decreases, employees may be furloughed. Suppliers may need to deliver fewer raw materials, which may increase supply costs. All of these responses to price change will inevitably impact owner and investor dividends.

E-commerce is sometimes divided into a number of different types. B2C (business-to-consumer) is the type of e-commerce we think of most often. B2B (business-to-business), B2G (business-to-government), and G2G (government-to-government) are types of commerce that are often associated with regular, high-volume sales. C2C (consumer-to-consumer) or P2P (peer-to-peer) are related to one of the oldest forms of commerce—bartering—but today, they are most often associated with marketplaces like eBay.

Value and Supply Chains

Every input and transformational process that contributes to a product also contributes to the product's value chain. A value chain is sometimes analyzed within an individual company, but it can also extend across the whole supply chain. (A supply chain includes the network of suppliers and producers required to create a final product.)

For example, making goods requires finding raw materials, mining raw materials, refining raw materials, combining materials into a prototype, refining a prototype, creating a final product, packing the final product, and delivering the final product to a customer.

A similar example of a value chain for a service would begin with ideation and might continue with the development of a static prototype app and then the production and delivery of a "smart" (data-informed) app.

In each step, the work done improves the value of the materials or ideas of interest. Adding value typically costs the producer money, but customers are willing to pay more for a more valuable product.

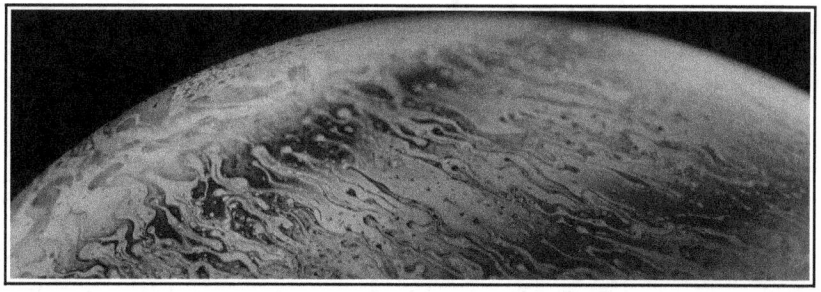

The macro business landscape is often hard to see, and in the first wave of e-commerce, it was difficult to see the bubble supporting the economy. The world did not predict the dramatic impact of the "dot-com bubble."

Section 1.2 A Brief History of E-Commerce

E-commerce has been conducted since the 1960s, not too long after the first general-purpose computers were built in the 1940s and 1950s and well before the first computers with digital displays were released in the mid-1970s.

E-commerce began with a set of protocols and technologies known as EDI (electronic data interchange). EDI is still used today. Standard formats allow businesses to transmit information and update shared records. An illustrative example of EDI is the transmission of common quotes, purchase orders, and invoices between different departments in a company or between companies in a supply chain. EDI ensures information does not have to be manually re-entered into an electronic record by every department, business, or other entity.

EDI revolutionized commerce because it decreased work while improving the speed and quality of data. There are a number of rule sets available for EDI, but a common one in use today is UN/EDIFACT (United Nations Rules for Electronic Data Interchange for Administration, Commerce and Transport), which was established in 1987. EDI is software-independent and can be formatted using protocols such as XML (extensible markup language) or JSON (JavaScript object notation).

The First Wave

Despite the enduring legacy of EDI in e-commerce, the first wave of modern e-commerce is generally considered to have begun in the mid-1990s. At this time, Internet adoption was rising, and the first e-commerce giants were born.

During the first wave, most e-commerce sites were simple extensions of brick-and-mortar stores. These sites were focused on retail and written almost exclusively in the English language.

There were few deviations from typical in-store business models. An explosion of e-commerce sites led to the "dot-com boom," which lasted for about 5 years. The "dot-com bust" came around the year 2000 when too many entrepreneurs and venture capitalists devoted money to ill-conceived business plans.

Pets.com is one of the greatest dot-com disasters. It had a lot going for it: an effective advertising campaign and a growing base of hundreds of thousands of customers. Unfortunately, its growing success, coupled with its poor business plan, actually accelerated the firm's failure. The company offered low prices and free shipping to build a customer base, but the cost of shipping heavy dog food and kitty litter made each sale a loss. Its sock-puppet mascot went from doing high-profile magazine and television interviews to wasting away in collectors' basements.

Although Pets.com failed spectacularly, sites such as BarnesAndNoble.com continued to grow (expanding beyond books to other types of media), and even single-product retailers found success (e.g., CuffLinks.com sold a limited inventory to a niche audience but grew to become a market leader). Many businesses failed during the "dot-com bust," but the overall number and value of sales continued to grow. E-commerce certainly lived on!

The Second Wave

As web sites expanded beyond retail and into the service sector, the second wave of e-commerce arrived. Web sites began to focus on reaching customers where they were. Sites made greater use of e-mail to connect with consumers, and they expanded their reach beyond the English-speaking world, using localization to reach a global market.

Localization—the process of adapting to a specific (often geographic) market—was driven in part by the growth of social platforms such as MySpace and blogging platforms such as LiveJournal. After minimal translation work for a site's controls, users could create valuable content in a wide variety of languages. More content led to more visitors and higher revenue from advertising and other sources.

E-commerce web sites benefited from new business models, especially subscription models, and they took advantage of infrastructure changes happening on the web to create richer, more interactive user experiences. Macromedia Flash was an early technology for creating interactive media, and ActionScript 2.0 in 2004 led to interactive games and videos, even with low-bandwidth Internet connections. The public release of Gmail in the same year also paired increased interactivity with lower demand on bandwidth. It used a new set of technologies known as AJAX (asynchronous JavaScript and XML). With AJAX, portions of web sites could be updated without refreshing the whole page, making users' experiences more seamless.

Although MySpace and LiveJournal have declined since

their meteoric rises, social media, blogging, and microblogging live on. Services such as TikTok, Facebook, and Medium reach millions of active users each day, but, thanks to the benefits of the third wave of e-commerce, they are more successful than at launch.

The Third Wave

Just as the second wave built on the first, the third wave of e-commerce built on the second. It added a content focus to those of services and retail. Analytics, cookies, and tracking enabled businesses to better understand their customers, better reach their customers, and better curate experiences for each customer.

Spotify is among the sites that have algorithms seeking to present what will appeal most to customers, offering recommendations of what to watch next, much as Shopify offers recommendations on what to buy next.

The third wave also benefited from an infrastructure change. Localization grew into globalization, and customers around the world took advantage of mobile devices to access the web. This did not just expand access to e-commerce; it also changed consumer behavior through always-on connections and the location-aware social/local features that were perfect for expanding content pools.

The shift to mobile devices led to responsive design in web development and, in many cases, led to apps that provided consumers access to business content and services no matter where they were. As the promises of 5G (5th generation broadband cellular networks) come to pass, consumer reluctance to use data may dissipate altogether, leading to additional shifts in consumer behavior.

Each locality has its own rules, but localities can shape e-commerce worldwide. For example, the EU's GDPR, California's Consumer Privacy Act, and Twitter v. Taamneh (2022) have all shaped consumer web privacy.

Section 1.3 A Legal History of E-Commerce

One consumer behavior you may be familiar with is the need to bat away the now-ubiquitous cookie-notification popups or banners. If you remember a time before these, you are likely remembering a year before 2016. That was the year the European Union (EU) passed the GDPR: Global Data Protection Regulations. The law would not come into full force until 2018, but among other things, this legislation required businesses operating in the EU to give users an easy way to opt out of most cookies.

It sparked similar legislation in other localities, including the 2018 California Consumer Privacy Act. Most globally operating companies chose to honor the most restrictive of these rule sets in order to minimize the burden of these rules on their operations. (Can you imagine trying to follow 262 different countries' rules, let alone rules from smaller government entities?!) One of the most visible results is the cookie-notification banner, which varies in appearance but not in purpose.

Of course, choosing to follow the most restrictive rules is not the only path businesses choose. Some companies who primarily do business outside the EU use a banner declaring that cookies are used without giving the user an option to opt out. Many U.S. colleges and universities use such a banner; they welcome international students, but all business will be conducted in the United States.

A path besides honoring and bypassing restrictions is product differentiation between localities. In 2021, Facebook was in the news when it declared it would block people from seeing or sharing news in Australia. This was a temporary response to an Australian law that would have required Facebook to pay news publishers to display their content. In lieu of payment, Facebook planned to disable all news features of their product for users in that locality.

Legislative Actions

All of the examples provided so far are examples of legislative actions: laws created in order to regulate the "world wild west" of e-commerce.

The Digital Millennium Copyright Act (DMCA) of 1998 was an influential early U.S. law that had a global effect on e-commerce. Every web site that publishes user-submitted data should have a DMCA notice describing who to contact if you own content which has been erroneously published (or pirated) on the site. YouTube's DMCA policy even allows preemptive upload of copyrighted audio/video through YouTube's Copyright Match Tool so its automated system can flag copyrighted materials before they are published.

Sharing of copyrighted content is one exclusion to Section 230 of the U.S. Communications Decency Act, which gives publishers great freedom to publish materials. Section 230 declares that uploaders are liable for what they post; publishers are protected from most liability. (Exceptions beyond copyright violations include materials related to sex work and other violations of federal criminal law.) Several U.S. Supreme Court cases, including *Twitter Inc. v. Taamneh (2022)* and *Gonzales v. Google LLC (2022)*, challenged the interpretation of Section 230, but the current rules were maintained in both cases. Other countries hold publishers more liable for potentially harmful content, and the EU's Digital Services Act is an example.

In 2023, the EU implemented its Digital Services Act and Digital Markets Act. The Digital Services Act (DSA) impacted 19 platforms at its onset, including YouTube, Google Search, Alibaba AliExpress, Booking.com, LinkedIn, Pinterest, and Snapchat. The DSA requires content moderation, transparency, and protections for minors as described by the law. The Digital Markets Act works in concert with the DSA to make additional rules for "gatekeeper" corporations that enjoy an entrenched and durable position in digital service markets, such as operating systems, search engines, social networking services, virtual assistants, and web browsers. These gatekeeper services are required to allow users to easily uninstall default apps, change default settings, and unsubscribe as easily as they subscribe. They are also required to allow third parties to inter-operate with the gatekeeper's own services and to favor third-party services no less than their own.

One final U.S. law to be familiar with is U.S. Code Title 17, Chapter 1, Section 107. It describes a doctrine known as Fair Use. You should have Fair Use in mind when using others' materials, even when using those materials in creative new ways. Fair Use has been better defined by judicial precedent, but the original law below sets out the factors that are considered in determining if use of copyrighted works is fair use:

"...the fair use of a copyrighted work... for purposes

such as criticism, comment, news reporting, teaching (including multiple copies for classroom use), scholarship, or research, is not an infringement of copyright. ...The factors to be considered shall include —

>(1) the purpose and character of the use, including whether such use is of a commercial nature or is for nonprofit educational purposes;
>(2) the nature of the copyrighted work;
>(3) the amount and substantiality of the portion used in relation to the copyrighted work as a whole; and
>(4) the effect of the use upon the potential market for or value of the copyrighted work.

The fact that a work is unpublished shall not itself bar a finding of fair use if such finding is made upon consideration of all the above factors."

Executive Actions

In addition to legislative actions, some rules applied to e-businesses are born by executive action. Executive action is how legislation is implemented, and implementation does not always match the written intent of the law.

For example, net neutrality is a concept that has only ever been implemented through executive action. In 2005, 2010, and 2015, the Federal Communications Commission (FCC) reinterpreted existing laws to determine that no form of Internet traffic should be promoted above another (for example, Paramount should not be able to pay an Internet service provider [ISP] to have its content delivered faster than a competitor). In 2008 and 2014, courts sided with Comcast and Verizon, respectively. However, in 2016, courts sided with the FCC in *U.S. Telecom Association v. FCC*. In 2017, the new head of the FCC reverted net neutrality rules, only for the rules to be enacted once again through Executive Order 14036 in July 2021. Over a period of 16 years, net neutrality was in effect for approximately half that time, as a result of at least five executive actions.

Other notable executive actions in the United States include actions concerning trafficking of illicit and counterfeit goods as well as avoidance of customs duties, taxes, and fees (Executive Order 13904, January 31, 2020) and directives to develop and manage digital assets (Executive Order 14067, March 9, 2022).

Outside the United States, autocratic regimes often implement executive actions to interfere in digital communications. Internet monitoring and prosecutions related to e-commerce activities are common in Egypt, Iran, Malaysia, Russia, Syria, and Tunisia. Burma, Cuba, North Korea, and Turkmenistan have limited the portion of the population with access to the Internet, whereas China, Iran, and Tunisia actively promote the Internet to stimulate innovation and economic growth. However, China, Iran, and Tunisia all conduct deep packet inspection to intercept e-mail messages, sometimes removing or altering content before it reaches its recipient.

<u>Judicial Actions</u>
When laws do not align with other laws (with the U.S. Constitution in particular), or when executive actions do not align with the law, rules can be challenged through court systems. As judicial decisions are made, laws may be reinterpreted, shaping future executive actions, especially those related to enforcement.

An early example of a U.S. Supreme Court decision that had an unexpected impact on e-commerce is *Munn v. Illinois (1877)*. Munn & Scott, a grain warehouse firm in Chicago, was found guilty of exceeding maximum storage and transport rates established by the Illinois legislature. In response, Munn & Scott sued for deprivation of property without the due process of law. The Court found in favor of Illinois, ruling that private businesses could be regulated in the interest of the general public. This decision has been tempered by other cases, such as *Wabash, St. Louis & Pacific Railway Co. v. Illinois (1886)*, but many regulations on private industry can be traced back to this decision.

In a similar decision, *Wickard v. Filburn (1942)*, Secretary of Agriculture Wickard sued Filburn for planting more wheat than he was allowed. Congress had established limits on wheat production in order to stabilize prices. Filburn claimed the extra wheat would be used by his family and not sold on the market, but the court ruled that even private actions can affect the public market. (In this case, Filburn would not need to buy wheat from the market, which could affect market prices due to reduced demand.) When the court ruled in favor of Wickard, it strengthened the federal government's regulatory powers through the Constitution's Commerce Clause (Article 1, Section 8). The court ruled that even if commerce does not take place "among the several States," as stated by the Constitution, commerce that might affect markets in multiple states can be regulated.

Rulings by lower courts also have an impact on how legislation is interpreted. In *Scott Paper Co. v. Scott's Liquid Gold, Inc. (D. Del. 1977)*, the Federal District Court of Delaware forever reshaped trademark law. (Trademarks are a form of intellectual property, such as a name or logo, that is used to distinguish one product from another.) By ruling that Scott's Liquid Gold was infringing upon Scott's Paper Company's trademark—marketing a product with a similar name in a similar industry—the court forced entrepreneurs to carefully consider whether business and product names could infringe upon other companies' property and profit.

> ### Intellectual Property
> A trademark is just one form of protection for intellectual property. Patents are used to protect a product design, feature, or method for a period of time (often 20 years). By protecting the results of research and development, governments seek to promote innovation, including through new ideas borne of old ones. Unlike copyrights, in which registration is functionally optional, trademarks and patents must be applied for and granted. Because applying for a patent does not guarantee a patent being granted, some companies opt to maintain trade secrets instead of pursuing legal protection. For example, many culinary products use secret recipes to maintain market dominance.

Lower court rulings can be magnified by higher court actions, even when the higher court fails to take action. In early 2024, the U.S. Supreme Court declined to hear appeals by Apple and Epic Games in *Epic Games, Inc. v. Apple, Inc. (9th Cir., 2023)*. In doing so, the Supreme Court affirmed a Circuit Court order that largely ruled in favor of Apple while offering an important concession to Epic Games: Apple was ordered to allow developers to use external payment processors outside of the Apple App Store.

National Cable & Telecommunications Assn. v. Brand X Internet Services (2005), Comcast v. FCC (2010), Verizon v. FCC (2014), and *U.S. Telecom Association v. FCC (2016)* all shaped the U.S. movement toward net neutrality and an "even playing field for e-commerce." (The latest action was executive, so this movement as a whole is described in the Executive Action section above.)

Prior to *South Dakota v. Wayfair, Inc. (2018)*, U.S. states were only allowed to require sellers to collect sales tax when the seller had a physical presence in that state. (States could impose a "use tax" in place of a sales tax, but that burden was on state residents, not the seller.) The *South Dakota v. Wayfair* decision overturned two previous cases—*National Bellas Hess v. Illinois (1967)* and *Quill v. North Dakota (1992)*—that established the physical location rule for mail-order retailers and extended the rule into the Internet age, respectively. With the 2018 ruling, businesses that operate online are subject to collecting, reporting, and paying sales tax in most states. In South Dakota and many other states, sellers with a physical location in the state, more than 200 shipments into the state, or $100,000 in revenue must collect and pay sales tax.

Google LLC v. Oracle America, Inc. (2021) and *Andy Warhol Foundation for the Visual Arts, Inc. v. Goldsmith (2022)* reshaped fair use as established in U.S. Code Title 17, Chapter 1, Section 107 (see *Legislative Actions* above). In *Google v. Oracle (2021)*, the U.S. Supreme Court ruled that Google's use of Java code in its Android Operating System fell under Fair Use, protecting developers who aim for interoperability between software packages. In contrast, *Warhol Foundation v. Goldsmith* has likely limited Fair Use protections for creatives; Andy Warhol's artistic expression of Goldsmith's photograph was not deemed transformative. As described by NYU law professor Amy Adler, "It is now far riskier for an artist to borrow from previous work.... Any artist who works with existing imagery should now reconsider her practice." With the rise of artificial intelligence image generators, all trained on existing art, many are awaiting the next court case to see how Fair Use will change further.

A final judicial action to be aware of surrounds the conditions necessary for electronic contracts. End user license agreements (EULAs) for the first software packages were typically noted on the shrinkwrap of the software's box or case, but new methods were required as Internet-based delivery of software and services became more common. Hearkening back to shrinkwrap agreements (best validated in *ProCD v. Zeidenberg (7th Cir., 1996)*), so-called scrollwrap and clickwrap agreements became commonplace. In scrollwrap agreements, users must scroll to the end of the agreement in order to proceed, indicating that they have read and understood the whole agreement. In clickwrap agreements, users check a box to indicate they have read and understood the nearby agreement.

As similar agreements became necessary on web sites, developers continued to use scrollwrap and clickwrap agreements while also introducing browsewrap and sign-in-wrap agreements. Browsewrap agreements are generally considered unenforceable because users are often unaware that they agree to an agreement just by browsing a web page. However, the prominence of the agreements and the number of times the agreements appear in the main body of a web page have factored into courts enforcing browsewraps. For example, in *Devries v. Experian Information Solutions, Inc. (N.D. Cal., 2017)*, the appearance of the agreement's link above the order button was deemed enforceable.

The design of how agreements are provided has proven essential in EULA enforcement, so the best advice at present is to use clickwrap and/or scrollwrap methods at registration, plus sign-in-wrap agreements (reminding users of their previous agreement every time a user logs in).

Virtual reality (VR) and related XR (extended reality) technologies are potential disruptors of e-commerce, but they are more likely to disrupt the e-commerce of tomorrow than e-commerce today.

Section 1.4 The State of E-Commerce Today

The legal landscape is an important part of setting up an e-business today. Like the larger companies described in the previous section, even small businesses need to be able to navigate laws, enforcement, and legal dilemmas.

When faced with a legal dilemma, businesses need to identify as many stakeholders and options as possible and then weigh the immediate and long-term effects of each option on each stakeholder. The best course of action may just be the best course of action for now, but taking quick, informed action is better than no action.

In the case of a jurisdictional conflict, for example, when one rule applies at a local level while a different rule applies at a national or international level, businesses have several choices to consider. Many businesses would choose to follow the most stringent rule to ensure compliance at all levels; however, if rules are in opposition to one another, businesses may choose to follow the rule set at the highest level of authority. Of course, a federal government may have more clout, but local enforcement may be more likely. In the case of conflicting rules, it is also important to consider the

19

strongest legal precedent, a task aided by legal advisors who should be consulted in such situations. However, when properly informed of the business's responsibility, accountability, liability, and due process effects on stakeholders, the best choices are often based on well-established ethical principles as much as the law itself.

<u>Key Ethical Principles for Making Decisions</u>
- The Golden Rule encourages treating others as you would like to be treated.
- The Collective Utilitarian Principle suggests making a choice that would promote the greatest good for the greatest number of people.
- The No Free Lunch Theorem states that even "easy" decisions have costs—sometimes costs to society. Often, there are hidden costs borne by the decision-maker.
- The New York Times Test asks decision-makers to consider the ramifications of publicizing the decision: if a story about the decision appeared on the front page of *The New York Times*, would it improve the firm's reputation or sully it?
- Universalism invites decision makers to consider the welfare of all stakeholders and to recall that all stakeholders are humans with needs and values.

The same strengths and weaknesses that existed for e-commerce in its founding continue today. Both brick-and-mortar outlets and e-businesses have a place, but e-commerce solutions are ideal for some businesses because they allow access to a wide range of customers and capitalization on niche markets. This strategy is known as embracing the long tail: selling low volumes of low-demand products instead of large volumes of popular products. Antique book dealers have been embracing this strategy for centuries, but niche products also appear in other forms. One such example is BREAD Beauty Supply, which makes products specifically formulated for women with naturally curly hair. BREAD's first venture capital round raised $6 million dollars in 2023, not long after a 2020 launch.

E-commerce success can be achieved with a smaller capital investment: a physical location is not needed. In fact, a single person can be very successful running an e-business from their living room or garage. Marketing, customer service, and data analytics can be handled by ever-improving software, letting entrepreneurs focus on creating new products. On-demand manufacturing and drop-ship fulfillment agreements can even mean that goods can be manufactured to order and delivered to a customer's doorstep without ever needing to be handled or warehoused by the seller.

Although there are advantages to e-commerce, there are also disadvantages. There is no storefront for visitors to wander past, and translating your site's visitors into paying customers requires skill and judgment that software cannot provide. E-business entrepreneurs also need a higher level of knowledge. Not only do they need to understand every aspect of their business, they also need to understand technology, marketing, and data analysis to make informed business decisions.

Machine Learning

Machine learning (ML, a form of artificial intelligence [AI]) is beginning to impact the variety of skills e-business entrepreneurs need in order to be successful.

Early forms of AI are often described as expert systems in which large sets of "if, then rules" allow subsets of human expertise to be replicated by machines. Although machine learning is the more dominant system in the popular press, many AI systems still rely on expert training, especially in the medical and financial fields. Training expert systems is labor and knowledge-intensive, however, so ML based on well-curated datasets may soon lead to fewer expert system-based AIs.

Through examples and non-examples, ML allows a machine to set up its own rules. ML can be applied in simpler cases of speech or pattern recognition, but it can also be applied in more complex cases such as natural language processing, computer vision, or generative systems. All forms of ML are currently weak AI or narrow AI in which the system cannot perform outside of its defined task. These include systems such as Amazon's Alexa, IBM's Watson, and OpenAI's ChatGPT.

Beyond the limited (or focused) functionality of ML-based AI, these systems are difficult to apply to entrepreneurship because they often require a set of technical skills that are similar in difficulty to the work they replace. Knowing when these systems are most useful, knowing how to engineer a prompt to get the desired result, and knowing when the result is of sufficient quality requires a background in business management, coding, and marketing. Machine learning has improved the efficiency of some e-commerce work, but it has so far failed to transform e-commerce as we know it.

The Fourth Wave

It is difficult to know if the changes happening in e-commerce have triggered or will trigger a fourth wave. We may be unknowingly approaching a new e-commerce landscape, or we may even be standing atop a second e-commerce bubble.

Will artificial intelligence revolutionize e-commerce? It hasn't yet, but generative AI is becoming more beneficial for content creators (including web designers/developers). With more and more ML systems being built into search engines, web development tools, and analytical systems, its influence is growing, and there may come a time when ML or AI can build a product or web site with little human intervention.

Will virtual reality (VR), augmented reality (AR), or extended reality (XR) revolutionize e-commerce? The jury is still out, but despite high investment, truly revolutionary content (and consumers interested in it) still seems to be a few years out.

Will gamification revolutionize e-commerce? Gamified customer loyalty programs have proven largely successful, but microtransactions that seem harmless have provoked a backlash in the gaming world. (The best example of this is microtransaction-based Diablo Immortal, which retains a 0.3/10 score on Metacritic, compared to 6.6/10 for the previous release. Of course, that did not stop it from earning Blizzard Entertainment approximately $100 million in revenue from Diablo Immortal in the third and fourth quarters of 2022.)

Will new customers revolutionize e-commerce? Seventy-two percent of Africans (750 million potential customers) do not have Internet access. Combined other populations lacking Internet access throughout the world, it becomes clear that there is still a sizable audience that could shift the scales of global demand.

Will surviving a pandemic revolutionize e-commerce? Although Africa is the continent with the least access to e-commerce by far, its shifts as a result of the COVID-19 pandemic have reflected those of the rest of the world. Online commerce increased from 20% to 50% (depending on the industry) between 2019 and 2021, and a symmetrical

20 to 50% of consumers planned to continue their online spending as a "new normal." COVID-19 also exposed problems in supply chains (especially cost-saving, just-in-time supply chains), shifted areas of consumer interest, and created a new emphasis on logistics after the sale.

Will a fourth wave of e-commerce be the loss of in-person retail opportunities? Historically, increases in e-commerce have had minimal effect on in-person commerce, but thanks to a pandemic, many customers only just discovered the extent to which e-commerce alternatives can serve as brick-and-mortar replacements.

Any one or more of these shifts—away from brick-and-mortar retail, lessons from COVID-19, an expanded audience for e-commerce, gamification, the metaverse, or AI—could trigger revolutionary changes that we could look back at as the start of the fourth wave of e-commerce. Or perhaps the next big change is yet unknown or even unknowable at present.

If we can expect that the next key change on the web will be most akin to the transitions from selling retail goods to selling services, then from selling services to selling content, perhaps we should turn to science fiction for inspiration. Could the fourth wave of e-commerce see a focal shift from selling content to selling reputation? China's social credit system, as implemented in some localities, could be a step in that direction. *Black Mirror*'s "Nosedive," *The Orville*'s "Majority Rule," and *Community*'s "App Development and Condiments" are all dystopian examples of where such a system built on reputation could go, and it is arguable that Twitter's (now X's) changes to its blue checkmark policy showed the importance of fair measurement of reputation.

If the fourth wave of e-commerce has begun, we are not far enough along to understand its implications.

For a 2-week period in 2011, Netflix planned to spin off its DVD-by-mail service into a company called Qwikster. It stands as one of only two blunders for a firm that has otherwise been an e-commerce success.

Case Study 1 Building & Bending E-Commerce

From April 14, 1998 to September 29, 2023, Netflix offered a DVD-by-mail service. When the service was discontinued, few knew it was still on offer, and even fewer remembered Qwikster, the short-lived Netflix spin-off which led to a similarly short-lived subscriber and investment loss.

In many ways, Netflix is the perfect example of a dot-com success. It was founded in 1997 by Marc Randolph and Reed Hastings, Silicon Valley entrepreneurs who had worked together at Pure Software to produce its flagship product, a debugger for UNIX software. At a time when most Internet companies were clunky translations of brick-and-mortar businesses, Netflix was not a translation but a transformation—of the local video rental store into an unrivaled national video rental service. Beyond offering DVD rentals at a time when video stores largely offered VHS tapes, without the need to leave the house, Netflix was able to offer a larger catalog of titles than its brick-and-mortar competitors while eliminating late fees.

Over 25 years, Netflix shipped more than 5 billion DVDs to millions of customers. In the early days, envelopes were stuffed by hand. Envelopes were later stuffed by machines, but it wasn't until 2010 that the service was almost entirely automated: machines stuffed envelopes, sorted and processed rental returns, and checked whether discs were playable or if they should be thrown away. This level of automation was an important part of the business's growth—custom-built machines made the work possible and kept the service affordable.

Custom algorithms were also important. When Netflix acquired machines to check discs for physical imperfections, the manufacturer's algorithm for what constituted an acceptable disc was too lenient. Although Netflix did not want to throw away too many discs, market research had taught them the importance of customer experience. To ensure discs worked almost flawlessly, they embraced machine learning (in 2011—long before machine learning would be adopted outside of research environments).

Netflix was similarly ahead of the pack in inventory management. To save on the need for storage space, systems were built to keep DVDs on the road. Each title was labeled for return to the service center that was most likely to use it next, and it was usually sent to another customer without ever touching a shelf. Thanks to the custom-designed, streamlined envelope, the cost of shipping each title was barely impacted by a change in destination. By utilizing U.S. Postal Service barcode scanners, Netflix could mail out the next DVD from a customer's queue without even waiting for a disc to be processed for return.

The company made smart choices from the beginning. About 2 years into service, as memberships increased, Netflix was able to expand its catalog, expand its distribution network to offer faster delivery, and replace its utility-based, per-rental model with a subscription-based offering (unlimited rentals for one monthly price).

In 2000, Netflix began to offer a personalized movie recommendation service, mimicking the staff recommendations that were one of the last competitive advantages held by brick-and-mortar movie rental stores. Netflix valued a reliable, user-specific recommendation system at least 10 years before analytics-based services would emerge as part of the third wave of e-commerce.

The recommendation system was imperfect, however, leading to the announcement in October 2006 of the Netflix Prize, a competition to improve upon the current rating system's accuracy by 10%. Netflix provided contestants with a snapshot of ratings data from approximately 1/8 of their subscribers.

According to Netflix, all customer-identifying information had been removed from the contest dataset and some user data had been deliberately perturbed. However, researchers quickly discovered that much of the data could be de-anonymized using publicly available information (e.g., IMDB ratings), in part because Netflix's selection was so vast. With as few as six to eight unique ratings, independent of rating date, individual users could be identified. In *Doe v. Netflix (N.D. Cal., 2009)*, plaintiffs' attorneys stated that Netflix had received notice of the broken anonymity within 16 days of the contest launch but that the dataset had remained available for the full 3 years of the contest. In addition to seeking damages on behalf of a class, the lawsuit sought to stop Netflix from launching a second contest and releasing a broader set of user data to include ZIP codes, ages, and gender. Netflix would later back out of holding a second contest, citing privacy concerns.

Between the launch of the Netflix Prize and the *Doe v. Netflix* lawsuit, Netflix showed it was looking to the future by introducing video streaming. In 2007, the service was available only on PCs using Internet Explorer, but Netflix partnered with consumer electronics companies in 2008 to enable Netflix streaming on the Xbox 360, Blu-ray Disc players, and TV set top boxes, followed by the PlayStation and smart TVs in 2009. Support for Apple devices and the Nintendo Wii was added in 2010.

As the streaming service took off, Netflix planned to split its streaming and DVD offerings into separate services, nearly doubling the cost for subscribers who wanted to maintain access to both. Within a few months of the 2011 announcement, Netflix had lost nearly 600,000 subscribers, and its stock had lost half its value. CEO Hastings could have taken these hints before announcing a name change for the soon-to-be-split DVD service. A month after announcing the DVD-by-mail service would be renamed Qwikster, Hastings retreated on the name change but continued with plans to separate the two services. In this way, Netflix avoided a common misstep taken by corporations exploring e-commerce—making a successful, simple service harder to find and use. Netflix co-founder Marc Randolph describes this as the "Canada Principle"—it may seem easy to expand into a new, nearby market, but it will inevitably be more complicated than you expect. Applying the same amount of effort to the company's current focus will almost certainly lead to better results than shifting to a new focus.

With only two major gaffes, however, Netflix has shone as a beacon of success in e-commerce history. Today, Netflix is worth about 300 billion dollars, a huge advancement beyond the original 2 million dollar investment. In 2022, Netflix was the top user of global Internet bandwidth (at about 14%).

Questions to Consider
1. For most of its existence, Netflix has sold services rather than goods. Why is it still best described as e-commerce?
2. In which ways did Netflix conform to the characteristics of the three waves of e-commerce? In which ways was Netflix ahead of its time for the three waves?
3. At the time of the Netflix Prize, the U.S. Video Privacy Protection Act read: "Federal criminal code... prohibits, with certain exceptions, the disclosure of video rental records containing personally identifiable information." How could Doe's reading of this text lead them to file a lawsuit? How could Netflix's reading of this text defend its position?
4. The Video Privacy Protection Act would later change in part due to Netflix's lobbying. Its 2013 revision allowed consumers to provide informed consent, including through electronic means, for the sharing of video rental records. How did Netflix benefit from this change? How did consumers benefit?
5. Is there any evidence Netflix is embracing a fourth wave of e-commerce?

Chapter 2.0 **Initial Business Tasks**

As you seek to set up a business, it is common to do so with a start-up mentality. A start-up is often focused on a single idea. The simplicity of a start-up makes initial business tasks easier, but it also obfuscates the steps your business will need to take on its path to success.

Successful businesses will quickly expand beyond a single product by offering variations of a product to capture a larger part of the market or by expanding to integrate other business processes. As businesses grow, they often explore the ideas of horizontal integration: achieving economy of scope or economy of scale through increased offerings.

Amazon.com has made great use of horizontal integration. Its catalog long ago expanded beyond its bookseller origins, and it offers a large number of services beyond commerce, including Amazon Web Services and services related to its Alexa virtual assistant.

Amazon has also pursued vertical integration: minimizing costs by controlling as many steps along the value chain as possible. Consider how Amazon's voice assistant (often on an Amazon device) can be used to order a product from one of Amazon's private-label brands. The order is completed through Amazon's shopping service, supported by Amazon's cloud computing platform, fulfilled at an Amazon Fulfillment warehouse, and delivered by Amazon's fleet of delivery vehicles.

Although we will keep a vision of our business's distant future in mind, we will focus on the first three to five years of the business's existence. We will choose a business model, identify the market best served, and craft a corporate identity, all using fact-based market research.

If you have ever looked behind a bar, you have likely seen competition at work. What you see represents beverage companies' business models— flavor, price, presentation, and other qualities influence consumer choice.

Section 2.1 An Overview of Business Models

All businesses are based on a business model. A business model has eight different components, but all eight components are not always formalized, and they can be approached through a smaller number of processes.

1. **Value Proposition:** Why should the customer buy from you? We will address value proposition throughout this chapter and into the next.
2. **Revenue Model:** How will you earn money? We will address this question in *Section 2.2: Choosing a Revenue Model*.
3. **Market Opportunity:** What market conditions provide an opportunity for your business? What marketplace do you intend to serve, and what is its size? We will address market opportunity in *Section 2.3: Identifying Target Markets*.
4. **Competitive Environment:** Who else occupies your intended market space? What are these competitors doing in the industry? We will address this and the next two components in *Section 2.4 and beyond*.

5. **Competitive Advantage:** What special advantages does your firm, product, or service bring to market?
6. **Market Strategy:** How do you plan to promote your products or services to attract your target audience?
7. **Organizational Development:** How will work be divided (and conquered)? What types of organizational structures within the firm are necessary to carry out the business plan? We will address both organizational development and management teams in *Chapter 3: Finding Stakeholders.*
8. **Management Team:** What kinds of experiences and background are important for the company's leaders? What of this expertise is already in place?

Answering each of these broad questions will help you refine your company's role in its industry and ultimately help you develop your company's identity.

Legal Structures

Before you get into developing an identity, however, you may want to consider the different types of legal structures available for businesses. The types of businesses that follow are available in the United States. They are described here in brief; you will want to consult with a legal expert before making a choice for a real-world business.

A sole proprietorship is the most basic type of business. You generally need not create a sole proprietorship; you are simply required to include business income as part of your personal income tax return. A sole proprietorship is a good option if you are operating a low-cost, low-risk consulting business. If your business name needs more information than your given name can provide (even, for example, if you want to operate Austin Smith's Coffee Beanery), you will need to set up a DBA or "doing business as." (Your state may refer to a secondary name as a trade name or assumed name instead of a DBA.) Setting up a DBA allows you to legally market your business with a name other than your own, to open a business bank account, and to cash checks written to your business name.

A partnership is the next simplest legal structure. A legal agreement is made between you and your partners, and a DBA is generally required. After an annual information return is filed on behalf of your business, your shares of the business's profits or losses are passed through your personal tax return.

A limited liability corporation (LLC) can be created as an individual or with a group of investors, mirroring either a sole proprietorship or a partnership. Its main distinction is in its name: your personal liability for your business's actions is limited. In a sole proprietorship or partnership, your personal house, car, and bank account are at risk if anyone sues your business for wrongdoing. With an LLC, the business's liability ends with the business's assets. An LLC can pay corporate taxes, or taxes can be paid through the owner's tax returns. It has the greatest flexibility of all business structures, but it has all the complexity of a corporation, and its structure cannot easily be changed after its founding.

A C corporation creates a business that is separate from its owners. C-Corps can make profits, can be taxed (at a higher rate) on those profits, and can be held legally liable. All corporations (including the S-Corp and non-profit corporations that follow) offer the greatest protection to owners from personal liability, but the cost of forming a corporation is high, just as the record-keeping and reporting processes are the most laborious. Profit from a C-Corp is often taxed twice—first, when the company earns profit, then later, when owners earn dividends or other income.

An S corporation is similar to a C-Corp, except that it may avoid the double-taxation of a C-Corp if profits and losses are passed through personal income. There are more restrictions for forming an S-Corp, and regulations for S corporations vary most highly between states.

The B corporation (B-Corp or benefit corporation) is a corporation that seeks to provide public good in addition to making profit. Rules for B corporations also vary highly between localities, but, generally, they are accountable for providing societal benefits and for being highly transparent in their operations. There is no difference in how they are taxed, so many businesses seeking to provide public good pursue a non-profit corporation.

A non-profit [501(c)(3)] corporation will receive a tax-exempt status when set up to do charitable work, including education, religious, or scientific work. They pay no tax on profit or when purchasing goods and services, and all donations are tax deductible, providing an additional benefit to donors. These corporations have higher accountability and transparency requirements. 501(c)(3) organizations cannot distribute profits to members or to political campaigns.

A non-profit [501(c)(4)] corporation is set up for social welfare benefits or as a civic group. They pay no tax on profit or when purchasing, and up to 49% of expenses may be related to political lobbying, but donations to 501(c)(4) organizations are not tax deductible.

Choosing a legal structure is an important first step in setting up a business. S-Corps, B-Corps, and non-profit corporations have many rules that must be followed as you develop a vision of your business. You should also decide early on if you will share ownership and how others will participate in decision-making.

Laundromats often operate using a utility revenue model—customers pay per wash. This is not the only revenue model that could work, though. Laundromats could be successful with subscription or advertising models. Would you watch ads if the machine time was free?

Section 2.2 Choosing a Revenue Model

A revenue model is the method by which your business will be able to make money (generate revenue) and stay in business. We will explore a few revenue models here, but many e-business revenue models are combinations of these models, with more models being created every day.

In the merchant model, a business acts as a retailer, providing customers access to products made by others. There are many examples, with categories including bit vendors (e.g., Apple's iTunes, which sells licensed copies of digital media), catalog merchants (e.g., U-line has a fairly static list of product offerings), click-and-mortar companies (e.g., Office Depot's web-based offerings are largely duplicates of goods available in stores), and virtual merchants (e.g., Overstock operates an online-only marketplace.).

In the manufacturer model, a business acts as a manufacturer, both making and selling the product, often at a lower price because they can eliminate the wholesale "middleman." Monoprice is a manufacturer that re-brands products designed by other companies. Honda, Ford, and many others manufacture cars and offer them for sale or lease. Oracle and many other software manufacturers make money by selling version-limited licenses.

In the brokerage model, a business acts as a broker, facilitating transactions between other parties. Brokers can negotiate fulfillment (e.g., DoorDash) or serve as a marketplace or auction broker (e.g., eBay), a search agent (e.g., DuckDuckGo), or a transaction broker (e.g., PayPal).

In the advertising model, a business sells ad space to other companies. This might be as contextual advertising, interstitials or infomercials, ultramercials, or sponsored search engine results (e.g., Yahoo!). Engaget and many other content providers make money with contextual advertising: placing content-related ads next to similar text, photos, or video. Forbes and YouTube are well-known for barring access to content until photo or video ads (interstitials or infomercials) have been viewed. Many mobile games use ultramercials to incentivize players to view ads: each ad earns in-game credits.

In the infomediary model, a business doesn't sell ads; instead, it sells information to potential advertisers. Nielsen collects data on television and other media consumption and then sells this information as audience analysis. Alphabet's DoubleClick is an ad information network that sells information about who clicks what ads. Newegg and many other retailers offer rewards programs and curated sales offers called incentive marketing. Finally, Edmunds is an example of a metamediary—they provide car buyers with data and analysis to help them compare offers between different vendors.

In the subscription model, a business collects a fee from users on a regular, time-based interval. Subscriptions may provide access to content (e.g., *The New York Times*), infrastructure (e.g., Verizon), interpersonal networks (e.g.,

LinkedIn Premium), or security certificates (e.g., TrustArc, formally TRUSTe).

In the utility model, a business collects a fee based on customer use. For example, Audible sells credits that can be exchanged for audiobooks, and Tracfone sells credits that can be exchanged for metered access to mobile phone networks.

In the affiliate model, a business suggests both products and where to buy them. Examples of ways to benefit from affiliate programs include banner exchanges, revenue sharing, and pay-per-click. Banner exchanges do not provide profit, but they allow users to place ads free of charge on other sites in exchange for allowing other sites to advertise on their web site. There are no great examples of dominant banner exchanges, but if you have ever seen a graphic ad for another company on a small business's web site, it likely came through a banner exchange. To make a profit, companies can pursue revenue sharing or pay-per-click agreements with other companies. Many companies that publish product reviews, including TechRadar, have a revenue-sharing agreement with Amazon. If you click through and purchase the product from Amazon, TechRadar will earn up to a 20% commission depending on the product category and Amazon's active incentive programs.

In the community model, a business harnesses the time, skill, and emotional investment of a larger community, typically with minimal overhead. Examples include open-source projects such as those managed by Mozilla, open-content projects such as Wikipedia, or voluntary-pay programs such as the Public Broadcasting Service (PBS).

Hybrid Revenue Models
The static models mentioned above rarely exist in isolation. Mozilla, for example, does not just use a community model.

The community model is important: Mozilla harnesses the time and talent of open-source contributors and accepts donations through voluntary pay and voluntary subscription programs. However, Mozilla also utilizes utility-model agreements with Google to earn royalties from searches conducted from their web browser. (Royalties accounted for 86% of Mozilla's 2022 revenue.) Mozilla earns subscription-model income from Firefox's VPN service and their Pocket Premium web app. Mozilla earns advertising-model revenue through sponsored tabs/tiles and its Pocket Hits service. (Combined, services and advertising accounted for 13% of Mozilla's 2022 revenue.) Mozilla also makes money from interest and dividends from investments as well as gains through currency exchange.

If you are considering subscriptions as your primary revenue model, you might also want to consider selling individual items or features for a lower price (but for greater profit than a comparable subscription). This may appeal to customers who may want fewer products without paying the full fee.

If you are considering setting up a brokerage, you might also want to consider generating ad and/or affiliate revenue at the same time.

If you are considering a utility model, you might also want to consider subscription or advertising models as well.

It is always worth looking at what models similar businesses are using. Business models are one thing we will need to consider when we explore competition in *Section 2.5: Conducting Market Research*.

College-age students are one of the most marketed-to audiences across the nation, but it sometimes pays to target a more specific market: university students, technology students, or technology students who like laughing.

Section 2.3 Identifying Target Markets

Choosing one or more target markets is one of the most important things your company will ever do. Nearly any product, when marketed to the right audience in the right way, can be successful.

As we continue into Chapter 2 and beyond, we will focus on bringing a single product to market: a pair of headphones. It is a product that could appeal to a large number of people, but there are already a lot of headphones and related products on the market. We cannot hope to successfully market our product to the wide market, at least not without finding success with a smaller audience first.

From a product standpoint, what could make our headphones stand out? Many headphone manufacturers focus on sound quality (e.g., Bose), whereas others focus on offering a low-cost product (e.g., Sony). Form factors could be important: over-ear, on-ear, and in-ear options are all popular in different use-case scenarios. Features are important. Wired or wireless? With or without a microphone? With or without noise cancellation technology?

Let's consider a traditional pair of over-ear headphones with the most popular common features: wireless headphones with a microphone and active noise cancellation (ANC) technology. The fact that these are the most popular features works to our advantage—it might be considered by a large swath of customers. Unfortunately, it also means our product does not yet stand out.

We can aim for high-fidelity sound, which will make sure our product is worthy of consideration, but we still don't stand out, and we can count on paying more for high-fidelity components.

We know our product won't be the cheapest on the market, so we still need another edge. Sustainability-focused products are rising in popularity, so we may be able to embrace that movement, avoiding the use of plastics or using bioplastics instead.

Say we have decided on the path our product will take —fully featured, over-ear headphones with high-fidelity sound that are made from sustainable materials. Who can we sell this product to?

Market Segmentation
There are four main ways in which to classify market segments, or the part of the market that you can best reach: behaviorally, demographically, geographically, and psychographically.

Behavioral segmentation considers things such as how the product will be used. If we expect our headphones to be used in industrial settings, they should be built to last. Use in high society might dictate a sleek, flashy, or minimalist design. Before finalizing a decision, it is worth looking at data sources that provide information about the usage habits of our potential customers as well as their purchase history and purchase reasoning.

Demographic segmentation considers factors such as age, education, gender, household size, income, and race. Given our product's sustainability focus, our target market is likely younger. Younger generations, especially younger generations with higher levels of education, are more likely to be concerned with environmental and sustainability issues. Younger, higher-educated individuals with higher levels of income and smaller household sizes are most likely to be interested in our product and are most likely to be able to be able to afford a more premium-priced product. Of course, before forming a strategy around demographics, it is important to look at data sources to verify that these demographics match the interests and behaviors we are targeting. We also need to know the approximate size of the population at the intersection of these demographics. This population needs to be large enough for a small portion of it to pay enough to offset our costs and generate profit.

Geographic segmentation considers rural, urban, and suburban categories, as well as influences such as neighborhood traits, climate impacts, and general availability of nearby resources and amenities. Our headphones may not be tremendously impacted by geographic factors, but neighborhood traits and climate impacts may impact design. If "keeping up with the Joneses" plays a part in neighborhood dynamics, sleek and stylish design might be important. In different climates, our headphones may need to be waterproof or have batteries that are well-insulated against extreme temperatures. Geographic segments may also impact how we choose to sell our product—online sales may increase or decrease the likelihood of reaching rural areas depending on other factors of our marketing campaigns. Again, purchase history and usage habits are important datasets to examine with respect to the geographies you plan to target.

Psychographic segmentation considers interests, attitudes, and values. We have already targeted the portion of the market that values sustainable living, but a greater understanding of related interests will impact product design (are these outdoorsy individuals?), advertising campaigns (buy our product with the Earth in mind!), and social media messages (we need everyone to embrace biodegradable bioplastics!).

The Library of Congress offers a free resource guide for doing consumer research in all these categories (https://guides.loc.gov/consumer-research) that is well worth examination. It provides advice on conducting searches and provides links to datasets that can be free or paid.

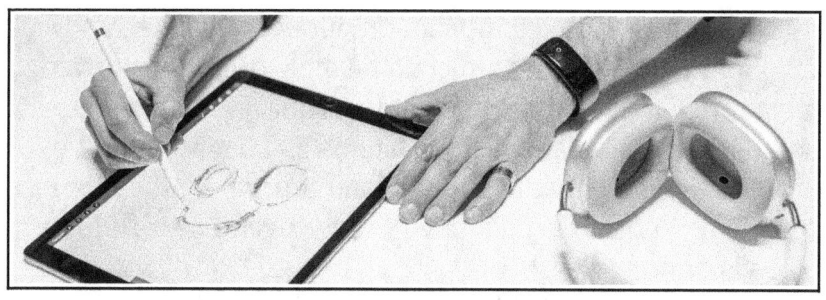

Which came first: the chicken or the idea of a chicken? Corporate messages are sometimes seen as unimportant "fluff," but without a strong corporate direction, it is easy for businesses to fail.

Section 2.4 Crafting a Corporate Message

When you have identified your target market and have data to back up your predictions, it is time to start thinking about the message your company wants to send.

Think about a few existing companies. What do IKEA, Southwest Airlines, and Tesla do? Why do they do it?

Mission and Vision Statements
Mission statements describe the company's purpose, and they often note the company's target audience and key offering. A vision statement tries to look into the future and describe how the communities they serve will be better off thanks to the company's work.

IKEA aims "to offer a wide range of well-designed, functional home furnishing products at prices so low that as many people as possible will be able to afford them" and "to create a better everyday life for the many people." IKEA presents separate mission and vision statements. The mission statement notes that design, function, and price are the three main influences on the company's furniture. Their vision statement answers the question "So what?"—because

45

furniture has a dramatic impact on our everyday lives.

Southwest Airlines aims "to be the world's most loved, most efficient, and most profitable airline." Southwest uses a combined mission and vision statement. They strive to be provide a service that is efficient and profitable (the mission statement). Why? So people will rediscover a love flying (the vision statement).

Tesla aims to "accelerate the world's transition to sustainable energy." Tesla uses a vision statement, bypassing a mission statement altogether. We have to understand their role as electric vehicle, whole-home battery, and solar panel manufacturers to fully understand their vision of a sustainable world accelerated by Tesla.

To write your own combined mission and vision statement, follow the steps below. Ideas for our headphone company are included as examples.

1. Explain what goods and/or services your company has to offer. *We sell premium headphones.*
2. Explain your company's values. *We are pro Planet Earth.*
3. Combine these statements into one clear, concise sentence. *Good sound doesn't have to be bad for the environment.*
4. Answer the question "So what?" Your answer should be ambitious and aspirational but also achievable. *We hope our headphones are so well-built that they will be the last pair our customers ever need to buy.*
5. Combine these statements into a clear, concise statement. *Good sound doesn't have to be bad for the environment: Our headphones are built to keep you listening for a lifetime.*

Each of the elements of the marketing mix—product, place, promotion, and price—should be based on data wherever possible. What data would you need to promote premium, sustainable headphones to apartment dwellers?

Section 2.5 Conducting Market Research

You likely did some market research when you read *Section 2.3: Identifying Target Markets*, but your research to date has probably been consumer-focused. We need to have a better understanding of the broader market landscape before we can start talking about our product or company with investors.

Marketing is the process of making strategic business decisions while balancing the interests of all stakeholders. Marketers exert control over the four Ps of the marketing mix: product, place, promotion, and price. These are the same areas we need to explore as we conduct market research. What products are already available on the market? Where can those products be found? How are competitors promoting their products? At what price?

Answering these questions will help us understand how possible stakeholders are likely to respond to our entry into the market. We can look at consumer preference surveys, as you may have done in *Section 2.3*, but we can also look at what our closest competitors are doing and how their stakeholders are responding.

Market Research on Competing Headphone Products

Symphonized Wraith 2.0 ($94.99)
Available: Direct, Amazon, Walmart
Promotions: None
Notes: *Sustainability-focused wood and steel construction. Well-insulated against outside sound, but no ANC.*

Sennheiser HD 450BT ($125)
Available: Direct, Amazon, Crutchfield
Promotions: Found at 50% off during periods of low demand.
Notes: *Not sustainable. Great sound, so-so ANC, 30 hour battery.*

House of Marley Exodus ANC ($249.99)
Available: Direct, Amazon
Promotions: Created with Bob Marley's family. Free shipping on all items.
Notes: *Sustainability-focused wood, metal, bioplastics, and vegan leather. ANC and sound are okay. 80 hour battery.*

Bose QuietComfort 45 ($249.99)
Available: Direct, Amazon, Best Buy...
Promotions: Found for sale everywhere, always with free shipping.
Notes: *Not sustainable. Great ANC, but only okay sound. 24 hour battery.*

Sony WH-1000XM5 ($398)
Available: Direct, Amazon, Best Buy...
Promotions: Annual launch events. Usually on sale for $50 off.
Notes: *Uses about 10% recycled plastic. Excellent sound, great ANC, 53 hour battery.*

Figure 2.5.1. Compiled information on competing headphones.

One option for conducting low-level market research on competitors is to identify the places, promotions, and prices of different competitors' products. The previous page shows relevant information about each of five companies' closest match to our future product offering.

One particularly telling part of a marketing mix is place. All of the products highlighted here offered direct sales and were available at Amazon, but being on offer at Walmart suggests that the product is made for the masses. Being on offer at Best Buy suggests a high-tech choice, and being on offer at Crutchfield suggests that a product is made for audiophiles.

The product that appears to be closest to our intended product is the House of Marley Exodus ANC (the model with Active Noise Cancellation). The other models are either unsustainable, barely sustainable, or are lacking important features. We are already targeting a premium sound, which is more than the Exodus ANC offers at present.

Brands and Competitive Advantage
A premium sound is our competitive advantage, and if we can offer our product at a similar price, the increased value is another. Another area we could seek to use as a part of our competitive advantage is customer service—House of Marley already offers free shipping, but we could match that and offer things such as extended warranties, money-back guarantees, or even offer 24/7 chat or phone support.

As you can tell, competitive advantages are things that elevate our goods, services, and brand beyond those of the competition.

Price and business model are often key considerations for a brand. Buying a car has typically meant a purchase through a merchant or manufacturer model, but many car companies now make money through different service subscriptions, including On-Star digital features, Tesla's Autopilot system, or BMW's subscription to enable heated seats. BMW's decision to offer this subscription in limited markets resulted in negative consumer commentary across the globe, but there is no telling if the up-front cost-savings might be significant enough for buyers to favor BMW.

A brand itself can offer value too—brands with "personality" have been shown to have the greatest brand loyalty and have commonly captured the greatest market share. Wearable products especially can use branding to get access to exclusive communities or communicate things such as values and wealth. People commonly stereotype based on brands. What do you suspect if someone drives a Toyota Prius? If someone carries a Gucci handbag? If someone wears a Carhartt jacket?

Toyota was one of the first major entrants into the world of hybrid vehicles, and as a result, many early adopters of hybrid, Earth-conscious vehicles drove a Prius. The Earth-friendly approach was a major component of Toyota's early advertising for the Prius, and it remains a part of their promotional materials today. Although the idea of driving in an environmentally conscious way is more associated with electric vehicle technologies today, no one electric vehicle brand promotes the sustainability ideals that Prius once did without also appearing to be a luxury brand.

In contrast, Gucci is a well-known luxury brand. Their promotional materials suggest the brand exists to stand out. Gucci's goods are often considered the pinnacle of fashion. Some users only value Gucci's high-quality materials, whereas others want to show off their fine tastes or highlight their life of luxury.

Carhartt markets its goods as workwear, which suggests that its goods are durable and long-lasting, enduring long hours of hard work in cold places. Carhartt wearers may perform hard work, but others may buy the brand's offerings to give that impression.

A brand message cannot become a competitive advantage overnight. It takes a clear corporate vision and a lot of work. People need many impressions of a brand before they start to pay attention, let alone attach ideas and values to a brand. Of course, brand identity is something that requires attention from the beginning. That is why crafting a corporate vision is so important, and why developing a vision should be completed as market research begins.

We have already decided that sustainability and sound quality will be the hallmarks of our headphones, but how can we communicate those brand values and attract the right audience? We will begin exploring these ideas in *Chapter 3: Finding Stakeholders* and continue this work in *Chapter 5: Communicating with Stakeholders*.

Before we leave the topic of market research, it is important to note that the sample research shown here just scratches the surface. Our customers and investors are the stakeholders who may come to mind first, but it is important to consider employees, suppliers, and any other party who is likely to impact or be impacted by our decisions. You can gather information about how all those parties will benefit from the choices we make in designing a product, as well as in placing, pricing, and promoting it. If you need help conducting research, you can turn to the U.S. Small Business Administration (SBA), which offers free small business counseling through its many Small Business Development Centers and partner organizations across the United States.

We will continue to develop all the components of our business plan as we begin to identify specific stakeholders in Chapter 3.

Although modern agricultural equipment does not look very different from the equipment of old, modern tools have new capabilities, especially when older hardware combines with newer software.

Case Study 2 Products Plus Programs

You have been making the same product for decades. What if you could sell that same product to the same customers but for a higher cost and with a service and subscription contract to boot? That is an important part of what agriculture equipment companies have been doing since the early 1980s. A simple manufacturer model has become far more complex, with additional revenue models including subscription- or utility-model service contracts as well as similar models for data analysis contracts.

Precision agriculture (aka smart farming) uses data combined with automation technologies to make farms more efficient. For example, precision planting leverages soil health data or previous years' yield data to place seeds in the perfect places to reach maximum yield at the lowest cost. Smart application of herbicides and pesticides can use data collected at the time of application to assess the need for the chemicals before applying them.

The adoption of precision agriculture accelerated in the first decade of the twenty-first century. Today, five U.S. states have precision agriculture adoption of greater than

50%: Illinois, Iowa, Nebraska, North Dakota, and South Dakota. At just below 50%, Kansas is not far behind. Clearly, the benefits of precision agriculture can outweigh the increased costs. These technologies can increase yields and profits with the same inputs or reduce the amount and number of inputs (including fertilizer, fuel, herbicides, insecticides, seed, and water), all while offering environmental benefits such as reduced soil runoff or greater ecosystem health. What a value proposition!

Especially as environmental impacts become more important in agriculture and agricultural policy, the value proposition may become magnified. In order to reduce, mitigate, and control seasonal fish kills in the Gulf of Mexico, its Watershed Nutrient Task Force recommended policy was to "complete and implement comprehensive nitrogen and phosphorus reduction strategies for states within the Mississippi…River Basin." If this plan turns into a regulatory framework, agricultural producers would be among the first to see regulation. If so, precision agriculture would be the ideal solution: by tracking soil health and yield data, fertilizer could be applied at different rates inch by inch in the field, ensuring no yield loss while minimizing the loss of nutrients into nearby waterways.

Of course, John Deere and its competitors are all working to provide precision agriculture equipment and services. They work to maintain a competitive advantage through technology, price, and revenue model. However, the greatest competitive advantage may come from another source. Because precision agriculture relies on accurate data, it may be the best data that leads to the best software and the best smart farming solutions.

John Deere, like most precision agriculture companies, includes data collection agreements in its contracts with farmers. The more data these companies have, the more they can understand the impacts of farming practices, and the better they can predict what levels of inputs will lead to the greatest yield for farmers. These findings are the result of in-depth analysis, often aided by machine learning, where even small correlations, patterns, and trends can lead to marked yield, plant health, or ecosystem improvements. Constant improvements can cement John Deere's leading role in precision agriculture technologies.

Across the United States, only 27% of farms or ranches used precision agriculture in 2023—clearly, not every farmer will spend the money required to purchase new equipment and pay the ongoing service and data collection fees that enable smart farming. As a result, most manufacturers continue to offer equipment and service contracts that do not include precision components.

John Deere's market research has identified market segments, including early adopters, slow adopters, and traditionalists who are unlikely to embrace precision agriculture. Early adopters are served by a full smart farming offering, slow adopters are served by cheaper equipment that can be upgraded later, and traditionalists are best served by bare-bones equipment offered at a lower cost. Excluding any one of those market segments would erode customer loyalty, so any decision to eliminate options for these groups would need to be especially well-researched to ensure loyalty advantages are not lost to competitors.

In the meantime, John Deere can take softer actions to encourage the adoption of newer technologies: highlighting the success of precision agriculture customers in marketing materials, sharing information about solar storm disruptions of older GPS units (a subtle nudge to upgrade), and continuing to promote next-generation technologies alongside family-friendly content for the next generation of farmers.

Questions to Consider

1. John Deere currently uses a combination of manufacturing, subscription, and utility revenue models. What other alternative models could they consider?
2. The greatest profit margins may come from early adopters who pay top dollar for the newest features. What other customer traits could be analyzed to better target this group? How can early adopters be segmented behaviorally, demographically, geographically, or psychographically?
3. John Deere's company purpose reads: "We innovate on behalf of humanity. ...With our role in helping produce food, fiber, fuel, and infrastructure, we work for every single person on the planet." Is this more of a mission statement or a value statement? How does precision agriculture factor into John Deere's declared purpose?
4. All companies are under threat by competitors, market conditions, and beyond. What are some of John Deere's competitive advantages? How can competitors overcome those advantages? What should John Deere be doing to maintain their competitive advantages?

Chapter 3.0 **Finding Stakeholders**

With market research in hand, it is time to begin putting your ideas together. Initially, we will focus on communicating with investors in a variety of formats and situations. The formal documents you create for investors can also be used when obtaining loans, appointing a board of directors, and/or hiring employees. Although they may not be shared directly, the ideas in these documents will ultimately impact all stakeholders, including customers and suppliers.

Next, we will conduct whole-business analyses. You should use these continuously throughout the life of a business to better understand your company's role in the industry and to guide future decisions.

Hiring talent is one example of an important decision. You may begin the hiring process long before your business is officially open or shortly before, but most businesses will need to hire employees or consultants at some point.

Finally, we will look at the role of privacy and security in finding and keeping customers. All stakeholders share concerns about these issues in modern society, and you are likely one of the more than 50% of Americans who have been impacted by a privacy or security breach.

When you have worked through each of the exercises in this chapter, you will have solidified your primary plans and objectives, and you will have identified many of the possible pitfalls for your company. As a result, you may have developed plans A, B, C, and you may be ready to respond to any contingency. You will also be able to communicate freely and comfortably about your company with any person in any forum. Are you ready to become an expert?

Every elevator ride is an opportunity. (Not to stare silently at the door, but to engage in a meaningful conversation!) The simplest form of communication with a potential investor is a 30–90-second elevator pitch.

Section 3.1 Talking to Investors

Whenever you are setting up a business for the first time, lining up investors is one of the most important tasks. Even if you expect your investors to be members of your family, you need to be well-prepared to talk to them about your business idea.

There are many ways you can present information to potential investors, but the three that follow are the most common. These formats are often used in tandem with each other. Investors who have heard your elevator pitch may want to see a short-form written plan (either a one-page proposal or your business plan's executive summary). Interested investors and government agencies will want to see and store a complete business plan.

Elevator Pitches

An elevator pitch is a 30–90-second pitch, or the amount of time you might have if you were riding an elevator from the ground floor to an executive's office. An elevator pitch includes an introduction of yourself, your unique skill set, and your business idea. It ends with a description of what your audience can do for you (the "ask"). Usually, the ask will come in the form of a question. "Do you think your firm would invest in a project like this?" "Can I send you my business plan with more details?" "Do you know anyone who might be right for the job?" The pitch as a whole should be conversational and use plain language. Avoid industry-specific jargon that your listener may not know.

The audience for an elevator pitch is usually a potential investor, but it could also be a supplier or another potential benefactor (for example, someone who can build your professional network or someone who can give you low-cost media exposure).

Whoever your audience is, your elevator pitch should be well-practiced and well-polished. The sections should flow neatly into one another, and it should be easy for your listener to summarize your idea, identify your ask, and explain why you are the perfect person to lead the business.

When you practice your elevator pitch, be sure to practice aloud—with an audience if you can, or aloud to yourself if you cannot. Practicing your pitch aloud will slow you down and help you hear awkward prose. If you know how long you will have to present your pitch, be sure to time your practice sessions. Recording a practice session will help you log the time, and playing it back will help you notice if you are talking too quickly. A recording can also help you edit your pitch for tone, clarity, and conciseness.

1-Page Proposals

A one-page proposal is a step up from an elevator pitch. Because it is written, it can be a little longer and can be organized visually (e.g., you can use bullet points and titles). It can also include artistic elements or letterhead. The proposal should fit on a single, double-spaced page with standard margins and font size. It is easy for a reader to fail to flip the page over, and anything more than one page will come across as an intimidating read.

A one-page proposal should include the same information as an elevator pitch, though the personal information should be worked into the text rather than be front-loaded—i.e., "I'm me, and I have a perfect idea" becomes "Here's a great idea that I'd be perfect to execute."

A one-page business proposal begins with your business idea, explains your interest in the idea (often the idea's "origin story"), and describes how your background will contribute to the business's success. Like an elevator pitch, the proposal should end with an ask or a call to action.

Be sure to get feedback from someone who is unfamiliar with your idea to ensure you have achieved the level of clarity you need.

Business Plans

Business plans are a more formal version of a one-page proposal. Business plans are longer than a single page, but much of that space will be taken up by titles and white space. The word count will be higher than a single-page proposal, but it may not be a lot higher.

Business plans do not have a set structure, but they contain a set of big ideas that usually include a company description, a summary of your market research, details about your product/service line, marketing plans, and financial projections. The plan is prefaced by an executive summary that describes the core concepts of the business plan—even if your reader only reads the executive summary, they should still be able to make informed decisions.

Business plans should be incredibly concise and organized with many effective titles. Most sections in a business plan are written in paragraph form, but a single-sentence paragraph would not be out of place. Business plans are often written in the "inverse pyramid" or "funnel" format, which is also common in newspapers. The biggest, most important ideas comes at the beginning, and longer sentences with more detail come at the end.

Business plans are written simultaneously for two audiences—one who will skim the plan to capture the big ideas and one who will read the plan from cover to cover looking for detailed ideas. Most venture capitalists and other informal investors will fall into the first category (at least at first), whereas bankers considering your business for a loan will fall into the second category.

Because business plans are meant to be professional documents, you will want to ensure your work is clear, concise, and free of any possible errors, especially mistakes in spelling, grammar, or other language conventions.

<u>Company Description</u>
The company description includes your company's mission and/or vision statements, a list of your company's principal members, a corporate history if applicable, and the legal structure of your organization, as discussed in *Section 2.1: An Overview of Business Models*. Bullets may be appropriate for principal members, but short paragraphs should be used elsewhere to describe the who, what, and why.

If your company's hierarchy is important, you should include those relationships when you describe (in one phrase or sentence) why each member is critical to your team. Members can be named (e.g., Riki Sato), or they may be identified by title (e.g., Vice President of Marketing). Qualifications (e.g., an earned MBA [Master's degree in Business Administration] or 5 years of experience) are usually included for named members.

Market Research

Market research describes the industry you are working in, the types of customers you hope to reach, who your competitors are, and what your competitive advantage is. It ends with a description of the regulatory landscape. Each section will consist of a short paragraph with a concise and easy-to-understand title.

The main goal of this section is to convince potential investors that you are not a stranger to the industry, that you understand how your business's strengths and weaknesses compare to competitors, and that you understand how laws, policies, and other legal matters might affect your work.

Product Line

The product line section describes the goods or services themselves as well as their pricing structure, life cycle, research and development (R&D) plans, and intellectual property rights. The first and last items are usually in paragraph form, but the others may be bulleted as appropriate.

The goal of this section is to give insight into your company's products or services in the past, present, and future. This includes current prices, price ranges, or tiers so the potential investor can see how your value offering will compare to your competition. R&D should consider plans for your product as well as plans for measuring customer preferences or satisfaction.

Marketing & Sales

The marketing section highlights how you expect to grow the company, including how you will connect with and stay connected to customers (e.g., loyalty programs, after-sales service, plus e-mail and social media communications). It also describes the prospects: the types of partnerships you might set up with other businesses down the road. These sections can be short paragraphs or bulleted lists as appropriate.

As with R&D in the previous section, be sure to include product- and customer-focused items when describing areas for growth.

Financial Projections
Financial projections provide insight into where you expect your company to be in about 3 years. Yearly income statements and cash flow statements are financial forms that describe net revenues, expenses, income, and liquidity. (For more information on these, see *Chapter 6*, especially *Section 6.5: Financial Analyses*.) Financial assumptions follow written and data-table forms of these documents, describing how key numbers were calculated. For example, a warehouse's size and location explain rental or purchase costs. The number of employees and their pay rate explains payroll expenses. Ad distribution and cost information explain advertising expenses.

All of the numbers should seem reasonable to any potential investor, but investors will recognize that they are merely projections. Still, it is recommended that your net profit be positive (a net income, not a loss) by Year 3. Investors will be looking to see when they can expect to begin making a profit or when their line of credit will be repaid.

Executive Summary
The executive summary should be written last so it can be based on the best version of your business plan. It is an even more concise version of some key sections of

your business plan, specifically the core product offering (product line), target market (the customers you hope to reach), and what drives your company (your mission/vision statement).

Information is purposefully repeated within a business plan. The information in the executive summary and later sections should match, but the executive summary should be shorter and not be merely copied and pasted. Identical sections suggest laziness, which comes across as unprofessional and may result in investors rejecting your ideas.

Businesses use SWOT analyses to understand their strengths and weaknesses. Weaknesses are temporary flaws; it is only by identifying weaknesses that a company can grow new strengths.

Section 3.2 Pre- and Post-Investor Analyses

The tools we discuss in this section are used frequently by businesses, even after they have been established. They are used regularly because the analyses you conduct today will remain valid only as long as your company and its operating environment remain the same (not long!).

SWOT (strength, weakness, opportunity, and threat) analyses are usually conducted annually or biannually, but they are often revisited quarterly to track progress. Similarly, objectives are revisited monthly, or quarterly, though they may be revised only on an annual basis.

<u>Defining Goals and Objectives</u>
Missions and vision statements can tell us a lot about a company, but they are very broad and often unmeasurable. Goals are similar: they provide direction rather than describing achievable outcomes. Goals often operate on scales measured in years. Objectives are shorter-term outcomes. They include explicit plans of action, and they are designed to be measurable. Only by completing a series of objectives can we hope to achieve a goal.

SMART is one acronym used to frame objective writing. In the SMART format, objectives are often best written in four or five sentences.
- **S**pecific – The actions you will take are clear.
- **M**easurable – Metrics can prove your success.
- **A**chievable – It may be a stretch, but it is within reach.
- **R**elevant – Work on this will lead to larger successes.
- **T**ime-sensitive – Deadlines will help stay on track.

Before we have designed our first pair of headphones, we can begin developing a customer base and promoting the ideas behind our brand. What follows is a statement of a SMART objective. Note that the S, M, A, R, and T are not necessarily presented in that order.

We want to grow our social media audience to 10,000 people (M) in our first quarter of operations (T). This will allow us to reach a large audience as soon as our first product is available (R). Between the company's founders, we already have 5,000 followers/friends (A), so we believe we can meet this objective through a series of campaigns announcing our product goals, introducing our design team, and announcing progress throughout the product design process (S).

ABCD offers another approach to objectives. The output is a single sentence with each of four categories present. Again, components are often presented out of order, but they must all be present.
- **A**udience – who will take the action?
- **B**ehavior – what action will the audience take?
- **C**onditions – how will you encourage these behaviors?
- **D**egree – how much of the action will define success?

After our team publishes 3 months of posts (C), 10,000 (D) people (A) will be following (B) our social media.

The ABCD format is more concise, but because of its brevity, relevance is often unclear. Relevance may be clear if the only audience is your core team, otherwise relevance should be added above the objective, usually in a paragraph that describes your company's larger goals.

In either format, it should be clear who is responsible for doing what and what success looks like. Objectives are just the start of the work; they should be followed up with specific tasks for your teams to complete. In the social media example above, your team would need more direction on what campaigns to run and what posts to write. These topics will be revisited in greater depth in *Section 5.5: Marketing Plans*.

SWOT Analyses

A SWOT analysis provides four different views of a business by examining the intersections between the advantages and disadvantages that are internal and external to an organization. This decision-making process is important as a brainstorming technique for new businesses, but it is also a tool for analyzing business health.

As the table below shows, each of the quadrants has its own definition.

	Helpful in achieving objectives	**Harmful** in achieving objectives
Internal attributes of the organization	Strength	Weakness
External attributes of the environment	Opportunity	Threat

Table 3.2.1. Strengths, weaknesses, opportunities, and threats exist at the intersection of helpful/harmful and internal/external to the firm.

Strengths are areas in which your company has

complete control and has developed (or will develop) competitive advantages. Strengths may come from physical assets such as production equipment, patents, or long-term business contracts. Like competitive cost advantages (another strength), each of these strengths can be easily quantified. Strengths can also include more intangible assets such as brand recognition, employee talent, and innovative practices/processes. Good relationships with customers, employees, and suppliers are also intangible strengths.

Weaknesses are areas within your company's control where your competitors' operations are superior. Examples of measurable weaknesses include high operating costs and inferior or difficult-to-repair equipment. Intangible weaknesses include manager inexperience and ineffective research and development.

Opportunities originate from outside the company, but they provide ways for you to improve your business's position. Within your industry, you may find new business opportunities such as expanding your product range, expanding your customer base, or forward/backward vertical integration. Opportunities affecting all industries may come in the form of favorable legislation, a positive economic outlook, or new technologies to harness. For both opportunities and threats, be sure to consider changes to your competition, changes to the economy, changes to society/culture, changes to technology, and political/legal changes.

Threats are environmental conditions that are likely to harm your business. Within your industry, threats may come from low-cost imports, new substitute products, slow market growth, or a decline in market size. Shifts in foreign exchange rates, demographic changes, and public health emergencies are threats that affect all industries.

As you are putting together a SWOT analysis, be sure

each item is based on fact and not opinion. Also, be sure that it belongs in the category where you have listed it. Strengths and weaknesses are those items that are under your control. If competitors are doing the same processes more efficiently, it is within your control to do that process even more efficiently. Opportunities and threats are outside your control. Only after you have begun to respond to an opportunity or threat can your actions become strengths or weaknesses. Be especially careful that you are not mistakenly identifying these solutions to threats as opportunities.

No matter the format or medium, job interviews are stressful for both parties. As the interviewer, there are many factors to consider, from candidates' qualifications and their fit with your team to legal obligations.

Section 3.3 Hiring Talent

Entire books have been written on the topic of hiring talent, so this will be a brief exploration that falls far short of the legal nuances of the hiring process. For more in-depth information, work with a qualified human resources professional or consult with an attorney. Although this text will focus on the role of the interviewer, much of the advice may better inform you as a job applicant.

What is your main goal when hiring someone for your company? Hopefully, your goal is to hire someone who can (1) do the work you need and (2) do it well.

In order for someone to complete your work, there are likely minimum (required) qualifications. When you create a job posting, this is often the first thing that is listed. As you create a list of minimum qualifications, be sure that you are being honest with yourself and with potential hires—if you will not consider someone who has not earned an applicable degree or does not have a specific skill set, list that as a requirement. Being realistic with qualifications saves candidates time applying for a job they would not fit and saves you time reviewing unfit applications.

Next on the job posting is often a list of preferred (optional) qualifications: the desired qualifications that are not deal-breakers. Preferred qualifications should be truly above and beyond minimum qualifications. For example, you may seek a candidate with a degree in a specific field but consider candidates from related fields. Optional certifications or previous experience that is rare in the field may also be listed as an optional qualification. This list helps applicants better understand the type of work they will do and informs them of factors that might influence their success in the application process.

A job posting often includes two other written sections: one describing the job that is available and another describing the company at large. The job description is an important opportunity to describe the role the candidate would play at your company. In addition to the tasks the employee would perform, describe how they would work within a team, who they would report to, and if there is anything unusual about the working requirements (e.g., non-standard working hours, travel requirements, or frequent interactions with special groups).

The company description can be short, but communicating the company's mission, the company's values, and a bit about the community in which the company operates can provide important background information for job seekers.

Requesting a resume or CV (curriculum vitae) is standard practice, as is requesting a separate cover letter and a list of the candidate's references.

The resume is generally reviewed first. A resume tells you about the candidate's education and experience. Begin your review by identifying relevant experience. If there are relevant experiences, you will want to read those sections more closely. If there are no relevant experiences, you may choose to move on to the next candidate. As you are skimming/reading, you may learn things about a candidate that go beyond education and experience. An incredibly disorganized resume or a large number of typos can reflect upon a candidate's professionalism, but if professionalism is not a key part of the job, you may choose to overlook those errors.

With a cover letter, you can verify that the candidate will be able to complete the work you need, and you can start to determine if they can complete the work well. The strongest candidates will generally be those who can describe their success in a similar role or who can describe their success in a variety of roles (even if they are not directly related to the job at your company). As you read a cover letter, pay attention to what the candidate has done and why they have done those things. You may learn what the candidate is passionate about and get an idea of how they have interacted with coworkers in the past. If a candidate's letter leaves obvious questions unanswered, such as why they left projects incomplete at a previous employer, you can either add those questions to a list of candidate-specific interview questions or shuffle that candidate's letter to the bottom of the pile.

By the time you have reviewed all the resumes and read all the cover letters of your job candidates, you should have a short list of candidates you would like to interview. Interviews are generally scheduled a week or more in advance with every candidate given a few options for times and dates. Depending on how close a candidate lives to your place of business, you may consider scheduling a voice/video interview or providing compensation for travel. Many companies are especially apt to use a voice/video interview as a first-stage interview if a second-stage interview will follow.

Regardless of the interview setup, it is important that you treat all candidates as human individuals (not interchangeable commodities) before, during, and after the interview process. Although it is not common, making contact with all applicants and informing them of the hiring timeline reinforces the value of each individual.

On the day of the interview, it is ideal to have a two- or three-person team conducting the interviews. Ideally, the candidate's potential manager and someone else they are likely to work with will conduct interviews, perhaps with a human resources representative present. Begin with introductions and questions that will help the candidate feel comfortable. Avoid asking yes or no questions; if these kinds of questions are necessary, they can be included in an application form completed earlier in the process. Instead, invite the candidate to tell you a bit about themselves and follow up with questions specific to the candidate's previous experience.

Some questions should not (or cannot) be asked in an interview. For example, it is not permissible to ask about age, arrests/convictions, credit record, disabilities/handicaps/illnesses, experience with worker's compensation, family, gender, nation of origin, physical features, race, religion/creed, or sexual orientation. Questions that would give information related to these categories are also barred (e.g., "When did you graduate high school" would suggest age or "what was your first language" may suggest nation of origin). You should also be careful about questions related to military service and organizational membership. Questions about discharge are not allowed, but asking about military education, training, and work experience may be permissible. Asking about social and political affiliations is barred, but you are welcome to ask candidates if they are members of any relevant professional organizations.

Lines of questioning that are encouraged include those related to a candidate's prior experience or those that ask the candidate to give their responses to specific work scenarios. Try to avoid asking about extreme work scenarios (e.g., "What would you do if a coworker brought a gun to work?"), though asking about a few challenging situations can be helpful (e.g., "What would you do when encountering a challenging customer?" or "what would you do if you knew a coworker was having a bad day?").

If a candidate has the required skills and experience, ask yourself about their motivation. Would the candidate enjoy working in the available position? If not, consider moving on to another candidate, or consider the candidate for a different position in your company.

Handling phone calls or other contact with references is outside the scope of this text, but care should be taken to ensure your candidates and their references are not placed in the uncomfortable situation of being asked questions they legally should not answer (see the impermissible questions above and review laws such as the U.S. Federal Educational Rights and Privacy Act [FERPA] that limit the kinds of information references can provide).

The Gig Economy

Before we move on, one trend in e-commerce that is worthy of discussion is known as the gig economy. Many fledgling businesses have become behemoths by hiring workers as contractors rather than employees.

What is the difference? Contractors work for themselves, not for your business. You will pay a contractor for their time (and expertise), and you may pay a contractor for expenses (materials or travel), but you will not pay any benefits (no health care and no pension or retirement plan). Your business also avoids paying some payroll taxes (usually Social Security and Medicare); the contractor is responsible for paying self-employment taxes instead.

A number of e-commerce companies have run afoul of the legal definitions of an independent contractor. Although definitions and rules have historically varied by state, the U.S. Department of Labor established revised federal rules in early 2024 to rely on an "economic reality test." In simplest terms, if the economic reality is that the worker is dependent on the employer for work, then the worker is an employee. This test includes several evaluation factors:

1. **Degree of control:** The independent contractor's profit or loss depends on negotiation and managerial skills. They maintain control over their schedule, workload, and workplace.
2. **Worker investments:** Independent contractors will generally use their own tools, materials, and equipment to complete the work, even if they complete work at your business's location. They will spend time and money identifying new clients and engage in both marketing and advertising work.
3. **Whether the work and worker's skill is integral to the employer's business:** Independent contractors' work must generally be in an industry outside your business's normal pursuits; for example, creative work for a sales company or logistics work for a creative company. If the contractor's tasks are the same as someone who is already on staff, they must be hired as an employee.
4. **Permanence of the work relationship:** Contractors are generally hired for one-time projects with fixed end dates. Independent contractors are not exclusive to a single employer; even if they return regularly to a business, they work for more than one.

Privacy and security go hand-in-hand. Physical security measures are often ignored (e.g., leaving doors or computers unlocked), but social engineering is another threat that bypasses physical security.

Section 3.4 Stakeholder Privacy

Every business interaction contributes to a relationship, and that relationship is partially based on an expectation of trust. As a business owner, you are responsible for the safety, security, and privacy of every stakeholder. Customers rely on you to protect their identity and financial details. Employees rely on you to protect their personal and financial information but also their livelihoods. Suppliers, contractors, investors, and other business contacts rely on you to protect their information, reputation, and all the forms their investments take. As a business owner, you are responsible for taking all reasonable actions to protect your stakeholders.

Stakeholder privacy relies on security, so it is worth considering your business's potential weak points and strategies as you seek to mitigate risk. The first strategy to consider is storing minimum data. If the data is not stored, it cannot be stolen! Do you really need spousal social security numbers, a list of former addresses, or other sensitive data on your employees? If you are not making a delivery, do you need a customer's exact street address? Of course, by not storing data, you have less data to analyze, which may impact your ability to respond to customer needs or desires (see *Section 5.3: Customer Relationship Management*).

Physical Considerations

Security begins in the most fundamental form: physical security. If private data is available only on paper, and that paper is behind a number of locked doors, it is fairly secure. Most information is now digital, which means there are additional considerations, but physical locks are still important. Most data centers are behind tall, steel and concrete fences with on-premises security guards and additional security infrastructure, such as bollards, metal detectors, closed-circuit video, alarms for improperly closed doors, measures for fire protection/response, and more. Inside the facility, servers are behind locked doors. All staff have undergone rigorous security training and intensive background checks, and even security staff have restricted access to parts of the building. Few staff and no visitors are allowed access with data storage media in tow, and all access by staff or visitors is logged and recorded on video.

Does this seem too extreme for your business's data storage? Data centers are often protecting the data of hundreds if not thousands of people, but even if you only store a few users' data on a computer in your business's offices, the same considerations apply. Only people who need physical access to the device should have that access. That may require you to keep your office or server closet locked, keep your screen-saver timeout short, and use a hardware key or multi-factor authentication (MFA) method. Access credentials should be limited to those with a true need for access, and all access should be logged.

After data cease to have business value, they should be saved only as long as required and then erased: digitally, physically, or both. Data must be erased or destroyed when a machine reaches the end of its life or when documents are no longer relevant.

Technical Considerations

Beyond physical protections, private data should be secured with layers of digital protection. This may include encryption, but when using encryption, it is important to remember that encryption can be reversed (decrypted). For data that is only used as verification (e.g., passwords), non-reversible hashing may be better. If data must be decrypted, double-encryption is an option: encrypted both at the software and hardware level with only a small impact on system performance.

At the system level, security updates should be applied regularly, and when an operating system or other software has reached end-of-support, it should be upgraded or replaced. Tools such as system-level firewalls, anti-virus, anti-malware, anti-spyware, anti-rootkit, and similar software may be required. Limiting user access in the form of system or file permissions may also be a technical consideration.

At the network level, firewalls are important, as are updates to and secure configurations of all networking equipment where data could be accessed or transmitted. An astounding number of routers are configured to allow access from outside the network, and even if you apply regular updates to your computer, it is easy to forget about firmware/software updates for other devices on the network.

DoS (denial of service) schemes may be protected against at a network level as well. DoS attacks usually create inconvenience rather than breaching security, but it is possible to use maliciously crafted application-layer DoS attacks to confuse server or database software and accidentally reveal data, especially data in memory. For more on mitigating these types of attacks, see *Other Web Hosting Considerations* in *Section 4.2: Web Hosts*.

Sociological Considerations

All the considerations discussed so far constitute a fair amount of work, which is why many companies turn to third parties who are better prepared to manage all of these security-related issues. Unfortunately, bringing third parties into the mix increases the susceptibility of your data to the final category: sociological considerations such as social engineering.

Social engineering abuses the human instinct to trust or the human desire to help. Social engineering can be used to gain access to physical environments, for example, by "tailgating": following an authorized person into a restricted area. Social engineering can also be used to gain access to systems by asking for a user's information (e.g., "We're having a problem, and I need you to verify your password") or by "shoulder surfing": looking over someone's shoulder to see sensitive data on screen, watch a password being typed, or read a code on a sticky note.

Phishing is also a form of social engineering. By tricking a user into clicking a link and entering their credentials in a legitimate-looking system, those credentials can be captured and used to access the real system with malicious intent.

Your business's private data is only as secure as your weakest link, but only a hacker can tell you what your weakest link is. Once you have set up physical and technical security, and after you have trained your staff to be wary of potential threats, you can consider hiring ethical hackers to do penetration testing and reveal needed improvements.

Entrepreneurs are often referred to by the names of top predators: tigers, dragons, or sharks. Good entrepreneurs need not be predators, but they do need the support of those below them to find maximum success.

Case Study 3 Concerning Sharks

In 2001, *manē no tora* ("*Money Tigers*") premiered on Japanese TV, to be soon followed by *Dragons' Den*, *Shark Tank*, and other localized versions. In each, entrepreneurs pitch their business ideas to a panel of venture capitalists seeking funding or other forms of business support.

Entrepreneurs most often find a place on the show by submitting an application, but some are invited to apply by the producers based on exposure through crowdfunding sites or social media.

When established businesses pitch their idea to investors on the U.S. *Shark Tank*, they are often looking to move from an e-business to one that can also be successful in brick-and-mortar stores. This is always a risky move because expanding to third-party retail necessitates a loss of control and sharing profit with one or more other companies. Money is one way to support this expansion, but so is the expertise investors are able to bring to the table.

After some establishing shots, each pitch on *Shark Tank* lasts 90 seconds—toward the long end of an elevator pitch. Because the format of the show relies on the investors knowing nothing about the businesses being pitched, the entire interaction before a televised deal or no deal is verbal: there are no written proposals and no examination of a business plan until after the televised agreement has been made. Of course, that does not stop investors from asking for details that would be included in a business plan.

Most successful entrepreneurs on *Shark Tank* share in-depth market research, financial plans, and plans for product line expansion, marketing, and sales. Each segment may be only a few minutes long on air, but entrepreneurs spend an average of 45 minutes before the panel.

In addition to probing entrepreneurs' business plans, investors conduct SWOT analyses. This can be a stressful process for the investors, especially guest investors. On *Shark Tank*, each investor is competing with the others. Depending on the business's strengths and weaknesses or the opportunities and threats they see affecting the business in the future, they need to quickly calculate how each affects their own risk/benefit analysis. Investors also need to determine if the goals and objectives of the business align with their interests and expertise.

Jica Foods appeared in Season 14 of the show, hoping to gain the support of an investor with experience in sales and marketing—a step beyond their expertise in manufacturing. Jica Foods's goals of broadening distribution while following customers' tastes to new product flavors met the interest and expertise of venture capitalist Barbara Corcoran.

Working with Corcoran after the *Shark Tank* deal, Jica Foods successfully broadened their distribution channels, launched new product flavors, and used both social media and live events to increase their customer base. This progress was likely made with more than goals in mind: specific, sequential objectives were likely written and completed.

For example, the following were likely objectives pursued by Jica Foods:
- As demand increases and production scales up, the production team will keep order delays under 2 days. *Following their appearance on Shark Tank, Jica Foods saw an increase in demand, and they needed to scale up production without expanding too quickly or shutting down production.*
  - Audience: the production team
  - Behavior: will keep order delays
  - Condition: as demand increases and the production team scales up
  - Degree: under 2 days
- After the introduction of a new flavor by the R&D and marketing teams, 50% of new customers will purchase Jica Foods products regularly for at least 6 months. *Rather than using variety to increase sales made to current customers, Jica Foods has sought to use new products to appeal to a larger audience of returning customers.*
  - Audience: new customers
  - Behavior: purchase Jica Foods products regularly (for at least 6 months)
  - Condition: after the introduction of a new flavor
  - Degree: 50%

In addition to meeting specific objectives, Jica Foods also had to hire the right talent (especially in their Mexican processing plants) and hire logistics personnel through third-party contracts. Throughout all of the changes they saw as demand increased, they had to take care of employee, investor, and wholesale customer data: maintaining physical and technological security of the information while training new employees to resist social engineering attacks.

Questions to Consider
1. What kind of information would Jica Foods have needed to include in their elevator pitch? What kinds of questions might the investors have needed to ask?
2. Even after a deal is struck on *Shark Tank*, not all deals are carried out. Although Jica Foods's deal did move forward, what kinds of things could Corcoran have seen in their business plan that may have given her pause?
3. At the same time Corcoran was conducting a mental SWOT analysis, Xin and Melissa Wang were likely conducting a SWOT analysis of their own. What kinds of questions would they have asked if they had the option to do so?
4. What are five roles that could be completed by independent contractors rather than Jica Foods employees? What roles would be legally required to be completed by Jica Foods employees?
5. Jica Foods sells primarily to retailers and distributors. If their sales database was leaked, how could someone use sales and wholesaler contact information with malicious intent?

Chapter 4.0 **Building a Web Site**

Once a business is established, the first place many people will go to learn more is the web. Even if your business is not an e-business, it is important that you take as much control over your business's narrative as possible. (Though, as we will discuss in *Section 5.2: Social Media*, this is not always possible!)

As with most other topics in e-commerce, you need more expertise than the average brick-and-mortar business owner. You will need to understand the implications of every web-based decision you make. So, as we work to build your web presence, we will examine your web site from the ground up.

We will begin with a discussion of web infrastructure: the physical infrastructure and digital protocols that allow the Internet and related technologies to function.

We will continue with a look at web hosts: hardware, web server software, and the related software or programming/scripting that drives the web experience.

As we begin building your web site, we will carefully consider what content to include, and the site navigation that emerges naturally from that content.

With content and navigation in mind, we will consider suggestions for visual "front-end" web design and options for "back-end" web development.

Finally, we will explore methods for recording and analyzing web analytics. With web analytics, we can better understand successes and failures with content, design, navigation, and more. With web analytics, we can also verify that we are meeting or exceeding the objectives we laid out in *Section 3.2: Pre- and Post-Investor Analyses*.

The web is built on hardware, software, and the talents of many. Data centers around the world are connected by fiber, copper, and radio waves.

Section 4.1 Web Infrastructure

An internet (lowercase) is a generic term for an interconnected network. The first internets emerged in the 1970s, but you are likely most familiar with the (uppercase) Internet that was created in the 1990s. The first recognizable global computer network was the Advanced Research Projects Agency Network (ARPANET). It was organized by the U.S. Department of Defense Advanced Research Projects Agency in the 1970s. It used TCP/IP (transmission control and internet protocols) to connect known addresses, but you had to know the other computer's address to communicate. The domain name system (DNS) was the major solution for the known-address problem in the 1980s. It was followed by a codified uniform resource locator (URL), the development of hypertext markup language (HTML), and, finally, commercial interest in the Internet in the 1990s with the launch of sites such as Amazon, Yahoo!, and eBay in 1995.

Although the protocols driving the Internet have largely remained unchanged, the Internet has grown tremendously since it became accessible on personal computers. Since the release of Windows 95, the number of web sites, the number of users, the number of devices, and the speed at which users connect have all grown tremendously. This growth has opened up whole new realms of possibility on the web.

A growing user base permits increased communication and collaboration. The prominence of social networks and the burgeoning open-source landscape provide great evidence of this.

Increased access to Internet-connected devices have led to web-based work and play taking place far from the home and office. There are new markets for consumer services, games, streaming video, augmented reality, and more.

Faster connections have led to richer content offerings. In the early days of the Internet, transferring a single image could take minutes, but today real-time streaming of 4K/UHD video is easily within reach of many customers. Today's server and connection speeds have even led to cloud gaming services, where photorealistic gaming is streamed to devices as video. This allows consumers to play even computationally demanding games on slow devices.

Not all changes to infrastructure have been flawless, however. With all IPv4 (internet protocol, version 4) addresses allocated by the international registry in 2011, web hosts should now be serving content to devices with IPv6 whenever possible. IPv6 was formalized in 1998, expanding the number of possible device addresses from four billion (2^{32}) to 340 undecillion (2^{128}). IPv6 also builds in IP security standards (IPsec) and more.

More than 25 years later, a lot of networking equipment is still unable (or unconfigured) to handle this newer specification. According to Google, only 46% of web traffic was using IPv6 in August 2024, with U.S. adoption at 52% —ninth place worldwide behind Uruguay (52%), Taiwan (53%), Greece (57%), Saudi Arabia (60%), Malaysia (67%), Germany (72%), France (73%), and India (74%).

Between technological divides, political divides, and other challenges to an open and global Internet, the future of the web is more uncertain than ever—will the infrastructure of the web support continued growth in e-commerce, or will ever-expanding filters and walled gardens limit e-commerce opportunities?

The Path of a Packet

Most Internet traffic travels as packets. Your computer is likely identified by a decimal IPv4 address (e.g., 138.87.50.5) and a hexadecimal IPv6 address (e.g., CD18:0000:0000:AF23:0000:FF9E:61B2:884D). IPv6 addresses are abbreviated with full zero values removed; e.g., CD18:::AF23::FF9E:61B2:884D.

Server computers also have IP addresses, but to reach servers, we usually use DNS. DNS translates an easy-to-remember text-based URL to the corresponding IP address.

If you type msn.com into your browser, your computer will contact a DNS server you have chosen (either by providing it manually or by accepting the DNS server suggested by your web browser or ISP). If local DNS caching were disabled, every DNS request would hit two or more servers: a root server, a top-level domain server (TLD; e.g., .com or .edu), and a domain server if there is a subdomain such as assets.msn.com. With a query such as msn.com, the DNS server will contact a root DNS server to learn the address of a .com TLD DNS server. The TLD DNS server will return an address for msn.com like 204.79.197.219.

Your computer will request a connection to that numbered server, negotiating with other computers along the way to find any path to the destination computer, even if it is not the shortest route. This is a "by any means necessary" process that works similarly to how you might look for a vintage automobile. You may start by talking to an established network (i.e., car dealers), but finding the perfect car may require reaching out to a lot of unknown people and a flurry of notes such as "I know somebody who needs a Shelby GT350. Can you pass this message along to anyone who might have one?" It is difficult to track each note, so, eventually, when nobody gets back to you, you might give up on finding the perfect car. The same occurs on the Internet—if requests time out, the web browser assumes the web site is offline.

If the request is successful, your computer will receive the server's reply as well as the route the packet took to find its way. Often, this path goes through 10–30 servers. Once a complete route is known, requests can proceed more quickly; the same path need not be traced again. Of course, a single web site may require tracing additional servers in order to request images and more. For example, the msn.com homepage will prompt additional DNS requests and route tracing for ad-delivery.net, ad.doubleclick.net, assets.msn.com, bing.com, browser.events.data.msn.com, img-s-msn-com.akamaized.net, login.microsoftonline.com, and th.bing.com, among others. Loading a single web page can involve hundreds of requests (msn.com uses over 300), each of which may need to trace its way through tens of Internet servers. Isn't it amazing how quickly all these transactions take place? Most of your web browsing probably seems instantaneous.

Disrupting Web Infrastructure
The web was designed to find an address by any means necessary, but each step along the route is an opportunity for all or part of the web content to be filtered. With the rise of governments seeking to exert control over the Internet, a variety of ways to block the path have been developed.

In North Korea, there is a single physical connection between the North Korean internet and the Internet of the wider world. This single connection can be switched on and off, and it is an easy place to add content-filtering software.

In China, the "Great Firewall of China" is implemented by software that blocks access to certain IP addresses or requests containing certain words. This software runs on servers within the country that are contacted before a packet makes its way out of the country. These filters can be temporarily circumvented by using VPNs (virtual private networks); however, because Chinese users often default to services provided by Chinese companies, most content in China is actually filtered by content regulation at Chinese corporate servers.

In Russia, the government has implemented a national DNS system that replaces (and prevents access to) the international DNS operated by ICANN (Internet Corporation for Assigned Names and Numbers). Russian regulators can slow traffic to specific web sites, disallow it, or forward requests to domestic equivalents of foreign web sites (e.g., redirecting requests for google.com to Yandex).

Traffic to a specific server can also be disrupted using methods such as a distributed denial of service attack (DDoS), as discussed in the next section.

IPsec includes security layers that would ensure packets are unaltered and private. Although IP addresses can be authenticated, the system would not work if IP addresses were encrypted. Full IPv6 adoption would make content filtering much more difficult, but filtering packets by source or destination would still be possible. For the infrastructure of the web to leapfrog national limits on a free and open web, a larger move toward a decentralized, privacy-centric Web 3.0 would be required.

For now, web hosts should simply be aware of problems

with unencrypted authentication and the potential problems posed by association with the nations in which their web servers operate. Even operating a server that contacts another company-owned server in a different country can have legal ramifications for a business, such as those restrictions on data transfer as outlined in the GDPR.

Few businesses host their own web servers, so you may never see the physical hardware that runs your web site. In order to shop effectively for equipment you will never see, you must understand server classes.

Section 4.2 Web Hosts

If you are feeling comfortable with the architecture of the web, you may be well-prepared to choose a web host.

Some large companies procure high-bandwidth Internet connections (measured in terabits per second [Tbps], or millions of megabits per second) and host servers in house, but most companies choose to rely on third-party web hosts. Small businesses, even in the computer networking industry, use a third-party web host due to reasons of cost, expertise, and an easier path to geographic distribution of datacenters.

Web Server Classifications

Most small businesses that are not serving large amounts of media (i.e., not video streaming services) will be well-served by a shared hosting package. Shared hosting packages are the most efficient use of resources for a web hosting provider: multiple web sites are run under the same operating system on the same server. As a result, the server's resources are shared between web sites—each site is typically guaranteed a certain amount of resources, with the leftover processing power and memory shared between web sites. Unfortunately, shared hosting packages do not allow administrative (root) access, and if your web hosting instance goes down, a backup machine may be unavailable.

If you need a greater level of control, for example, to install and configure your own software, the next most affordable option is a virtual private server (VPS). These plans are perfect for web sites with especially complex applications, large amounts of encryption/decryption, and where security is paramount. With a VPS, multiple web sites still run on the same machine, but each web site runs inside its own containerized operating system. Again, each site is usually guaranteed a certain amount of resources, but you can usually pay extra to get access to greater processing power or memory as your web site requires. Because your web site is still coming from a single server, if your site goes down, a backup machine may not be available.

If you do not like the idea of sharing at all, you can also consider a dedicated web server. Dedicated web servers are more often built on site today, but they are still available through third-party web hosts. With dedicated servers, you have the ultimate in security and access because you control the whole machine with access to the high bandwidth and management services of the third party. Of course, your web site still comes from a single server. If your site goes down, a backup machine may not be available.

Without running multiple VPS or dedicated web servers, cloud computing is the only option that provides (nearly) perfect resilience. With the cloud, your web site is hosted from resources on one of several servers at one of several data centers. It is perfect for high-demand applications such as video streaming, though it may not be the cheapest option. Cloud computing maximizes performance, but you pay a premium to ensure all visitors have the fastest service possible. With other forms of web hosting, data is served quickly to everyone as resources allow, but if resources are not available, responses are delayed. Although not ideal, a slight delay is often acceptable, and it is almost always cheaper than cloud servers' utility model.

There are other variations of web site hosting packages, such as those that provide web site builders only. With platforms such as WordPress, the web host need not provide the versatility of back-end access, simplifying infrastructure and potentially improving security. The level of functionality is often enough for simple web sites and web stores, and some of the cost savings can be passed on to the customer.

Other Hosting Considerations
There are a number of web host enhancements that may come standard or may be available for an added fee.

SSL Certificates
Verifiable certificates are required to offer your web site in an encrypted format. (SSL (secure socket layer) certificates are now TLS (transport layer security) certificates, but SSL is still the most oft-used term.) If you want your site to be trusted and to avoid a drop in search engine rankings, a certificate is a must. Free providers exist, but paid options are simpler to use.

Processors / Memory
Increased resources for your server may be available for an additional fee. Directly comparing two server packages may require you to include a fee for greater processing power or greater system memory in the cost of one or more packages.

Bandwidth / Data Caps
Some web hosts will measure the bandwidth utilized by your site, either to charge by use or to throttle demanding web sites.

Storage
Unless you are hosting many large videos, most web hosting packages will fit your needs. If you need large amounts of storage, some web hosts offer storage upgrades or unlimited storage options.

Storage Medium
Most servers store data on spinning hard disk drives. For access that is three times faster on average, you can upgrade to solid-state drives.

Redundancy
Your web site may be synchronized between two or more servers to ensure it is available even in the case of a power outage or hardware failure.

Geographic Distribution
A step beyond redundancy, your web site may be synchronized between servers on opposites ends of the North American continent or between continents. If a user can access a geographically closer server, they can usually load your web site faster.

Content Delivery Networks (CDNs)
Instead of duplicating your whole server across geographies, the static (unchanging) files on your web site can be selectively served from cloud servers. By serving image and video files from servers that are geographically closer to the user, these larger files can

be delivered quickly to the user, with dynamic content still coming from your main server(s).

Backups

Automated or manual backups/archives may be available, usually with a limited time duration (e.g., 30 days of backups) and/or with a separate charge based on the number of bytes stored.

Operating System

Due to its low price (free!) and low resource requirements, Linux servers are standard across the industry. Windows Server equivalents are usually available at ~$4–10 more per month to cover licenses and other fees.

Domains and Subdomains

Domains (e.g., camelcamelcamel.com) have a low annual fee that pays in part for ICANN's DNS system. Some web hosting companies provide one free domain registration (perpetually or for the first year) when you begin your contract. If bought separately, a domain that has never been reserved costs around $20 a year. Domains that have been used previously may be "parked" by their owners—available, but with an added up-front cost. Subdomains are additional dot-delimited domains, (e.g., maps.google.com or mail.google.com). Setting up a small number of subdomains to direct to different web content is usually free, but fees are charged for larger numbers of subdomains.

Malware Scanning and/or Certificates

Privacy and security certification programs are rarely free. Services such as TrustArc will test your site and provide a daily certificate. Such a certificate may inspire customer confidence, especially in new brands.

DDoS Protection

Distributed denial-of-service (DDoS) attacks are becoming commonplace. Hackers use computers under their command to flood a server with requests to slow down its response time and potentially overwhelm the server's bandwidth, the server's firewall, or another server-based application. DDoS protection or mitigation services come in the form of separate servers that effectively add a layer to your server's firewall. These DDoS protection servers have increased resources dedicated to ensuring your main server does not get overrun.

Technical Support

Many web hosts offer some amount of free technical support, either for infrastructure or application problems. Infrastructure support is more common because such problems usually arise on the web host's end, but application-level support can be valuable, especially for novice web developers.

Navigating the web can be an exercise in frustration. Two paths may take you to the same place, but its impossible to know until you start down one. Many web sites can benefit from clearer, better thought-out signposts.

Section 4.3 Web Navigation

When you have established your vision for your business, it is time to begin envisioning your web site. This is perhaps the most important stage of building your web site because a strong user interface (UI) and user experience (UX) begin with a well-developed navigation system.

The first step is to decide on the menu items users will see and what order they will be in. Core questions to answer with your menu items include:
- What is the main purpose of your web site?
- What will users be looking for when they arrive?
- What else do you want users to do?

Most businesses' web sites will include menu items related to goods or services, information about the company, and contact information or location. Avoid multi-level menu structures: They can be overwhelming to users, and if we do not have a long list of offerings, it should not be necessary.

Additional questions to consider when creating a menu include the following:
- How often will an average user visit your site? Do their needs change if they visit more than once?

- What kind of experience, expertise, and expectations will your users bring to their visit?
- What cultural or language barriers could influence your users' visit?
- How much time or money do you have to invest in advanced content or functionality?
- How will users find your site?

Each of these items may require you to reconsider the available menu options. First-time users may need to create an account, and returning users may need to log in, so both options would need to be visible. The vocabulary you use and the functionality you offer may depend on the expected user population and your ability to provide in-depth user experiences. You should also consider the vocabulary that users would use in web searches—if those words occur in your navigation, your search engine rankings may rise.

If we consider our headphone-manufacturing business, it will be important for our web site to provide product information, information specific to our sustainable practices, and product support. The first of these pages could be simplified to read "Products" if we have many products or "The Perfect Headphones" if we only have one offering. "Sustainability" is likely the simplest menu option, but if we have the screen space, "Our Sustainable Process" may work well. If we wanted to highlight our corporate vision and other factors, such as a low-cost model, we might instead create a page like "Our Values," but this may be less impactful from a search engine optimization (SEO) perspective. "Support" and "Contact" are likely valuable as separate menu items, though they may ultimately link to different parts of the same page.

A web site's plan often includes wireframes, or basic visual layouts of the user interface. Sometimes these are hand-drawn, but often they are built digitally. In some cases, a functional web site is only a few clicks away.

Section 4.4 Web Design

With a menu in mind, it is time to think more about what the web site will actually look like. This process is usually begun by contemplating a few additional questions about the average visitor:

- What device form factor will they use more often? Although we can accommodate both desktop and mobile browsing, starting with a focus on one design may be easier.
- What is their connection speed? Users with slower connections may prefer fewer images and videos.
- What are their accessibility needs? Auditory, cognitive, physical, and visual challenges should always be considered, but if there is a large population of users facing a single challenge, those needs may come foremost in the design process.

With your menu and these considerations in mind, it is time to place the navigation on the page. In a desktop experience, a menu of The Perfect Headphones, Sustainability, Support, and Contact would fit well on one horizontal line across the top of the page. In a mobile format, Headphones,

Sustainability, Support, and Contact would fit well, especially if allowed to spread across two rows.

The navigation tells users what they can do. It works best when prominently located, clearly and concisely titled, and with nearby icons, as appropriate. When the user has changed pages, it is important for them to know where they are. It is a good idea to include an easy-to-find page title in your general design. If your navigation has multiple levels, you should include breadcrumbs that let them navigate up a level or back to the main page. (For example, if our company produced many different types of headphones, the product detail page might include breadcrumbs like Products > Wireless Headphones > Model A.)

Creating Wireframes

With navigation in place, it is time to create wireframes. These may be hand-drawn or they can be put together digitally. Digital work can be completed using simple tools such as a word processor or slide-show editor, intermediate tools such as Inkscape or Adobe Illustrator, or more advanced tools such as Adobe XD or Penpot.

Wireframes and mockups can be created at different fidelities. A low-fidelity example omits a lot of details whereas a high-fidelity example looks like the finished product. Fidelity can include breadth (how many of the final features are included), depth (how complete the features are), look (whether the example looks sketchy or polished), and feel (how close the example is to interacting with the final site).

The goal of creating wireframes is to understand the user experience (UX) when content is put in different places. Wireframes encourage you to explore the visual hierarchy of each page and to evaluate design principles such as balance, contrast, and scale.

The example that follows is a mid-fidelity desktop wireframe with sample words (instead of mere lines indicating words to come) but no actual imagery. There is no color—design elements should be finalized in the wireframe stage before you explore the role of color in a mockup.

The example shows vertical balance between the dark top of the page and the dark bottom of the page and shows horizontal balance between the text and picture. Even the bold page title and the buy button exhibit some balance.

The example also shows good use of contrast—the user is not likely to miss the logo or horizontal menus.

The most important elements are bigger and bolder with less important elements at a lesser scale.

Figure 4.4.1. A mid-fidelity wireframe of a desktop-sized website for The Perfect Headphone Company. Note the use of a footer to provide secondary access to navigation and instant access to contact information.

The example also follows a few other best practices. It places the corporate logo in the top center (the top left would also make sense for users who are accustomed to left-to-right written languages). Equally importantly, the most important information is available to users without having to scroll. Nothing about the web site seems particularly innovative at the moment, but novelty is only cool until it gets in the way of the user finding what they need. As Marc Randolph said, "A general rule of web design is that if you have to explain [how] something [works], you've already lost."

This site is simple enough to need only one page template. Some larger businesses may have two or three templates. For example, your homepage, list view, and product detail pages may be variations on the same general style.

Creating Mockups

Once everyone on your team is happy with the web site's wireframes, it is time to graduate to a mockup. This is almost always done digitally because it uses digital assets and because it is a step toward a fully functional web site. A mockup is used to explore the role of color, shape, and imagery on the web site. Mockups may also explore the role of font families, font weights, and font sizes. Real words may or may not be used ("Lorem ipsum" stand-in text is common), but real images (or at least approximations of them) will be used.

Multiple mockups are prepared using the same tools as a digital wireframe, or they may be prepared in WYSIWYG (what you see is what you get) web editors such as Adobe Dreamweaver or SeaMonkey Composer. As mockups are prepared, ask yourself what you like and dislike about each. Designs will inevitably be compared to one another, but it is best to focus on the pros and cons of each in isolation first. Continue evaluating designs and gathering suggestions until you have a few designs that you think are close to ideal.

When mockups are complete, it is time to gather initial user input. It is easy for business owners and operators to get caught up in their work and to over- or under-develop a design without taking user experience into consideration. Ask potential users what they like and dislike about your best few mockups. Also ask, "What would you do on this page," or "why would you trust/distrust this site?"

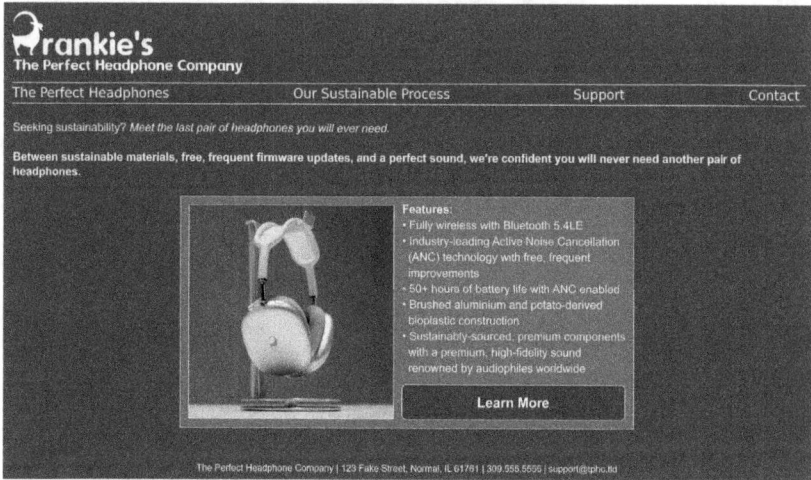

Figure 4.4.2. A basic mockup of a web site that features a top-left aligned logo, a header menu spanning the width of the page, and a prominent box in contrasting colors to describe the flagship product and encourage visitors to learn more.

Remember to compare and contrast the mockups only after analyzing each independently.

Figure 4.4.3. Another mockup features a top-center aligned logo and the same header menu spanning the width of the page. A large image of the flagship product appears on the left, and information about the product appears on the right side of the page, with gentle gradients behind the logo and through the center of the descriptive text.

Figure 4.4.4. A third mockup includes the same elements as the earlier ones but with a large image of a person enjoying the headphones on the right side of the page. Due to the prominence of the photo, the page layout has changed, with the logo in the top left, a more compressed horizontal menu, and an overall appearance reminiscent of a poster.

Creating Prototypes

The last step in the web design journey is creating a semi-functional prototype. In this version, built with your final web design tools, dynamic visuals are just as important as static visuals. Buttons and other items should respond to the user's hover in desktop designs if that is what you want in the final web site. Checkboxes, radio buttons, and selection drop-downs should all respond to the user's tap. If choosing one form field will reveal another hidden one, that should occur as well.

After web design (which focuses on visual design and user interface) comes web development. Web developers help the user experience come to life by combining visuals with front- and back-end code.

Section 4.5 Web Development

Web development, especially for small businesses, may encompass four primary skill sets:
- the visual design processes that might otherwise be performed by a web designer;
- the writing/photography/videography processes that might otherwise be performed by a content developer, writer, photographer, or videographer;
- the computer networking tasks that might otherwise be performed by a network technician or cybersecurity expert; and
- the front-end and back-end coding skills required of a true web developer.

Smaller areas of expertise can include:
- Search engine optimization (SEO), or modifying content and code to best be machine-searchable, especially by dominant search engine robots.
- Web accessibility, or modifying content and code to be machine-read or read by individuals with visual, auditory, movement, or cognitive impairments.

Because we have already explored web design and will explore content development in the next chapter, this section will focus on the coding work that occurs between a final web design and the implementation of web analytics.

Front-end development refers to the work required to create visual aspects of the web page and to make them fully interactive. Front-end work is completed using HTML (hypertext markup language), CSS (cascading style sheets), and JavaScript. These are also referred to as client-side languages because these will be interpreted by the user's web browser, not by any equipment under the web host's control.

Back-end development refers to the work required for data to be processed on the server before any data is sent to the user. Back-end development usually involves database integration and pre-processing using platforms such as PHP (hypertext preprocessor), ASP.NET (active server pages), Ruby, Java, or Python. Back-end development may not be required for purely informational web sites, but any site that allows a user to log in will require back-end work.

It is common for web developers to focus on either front-end or back-end coding; however, most developers have some knowledge in both areas.

Web Server Software Stacks

Running a web site requires, at minimum, an operating system (OS) and web server software. These form the base of a web host's software stack. As we will see, additional layers can be added to the stack.

As of August 2024, 86% of web sites were using Unix-based operating systems (including Linux). Windows was powering 15% of the web sites whose operating systems we know.

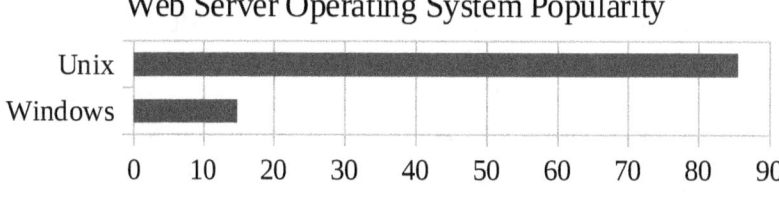

Figure 4.5.1. Windows has a market share of less than one fifth.

At the same time, 34% of servers were running Nginx as the web server software, 29% were running Apache, and 23% were running a version of Nginx modified by Cloudflare. Fourteen percent were running LiteSpeed, and Microsoft's IIS (Internet Information Service) was running 5% of the servers whose software we know.

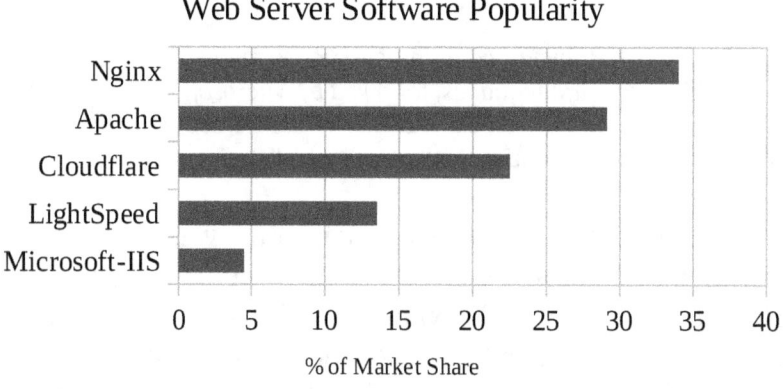

Figure 4.5.2. Nginx has held the web server software lead for several years, especially if you consider that Cloudflare Server is Nginx-based.

In addition to an operating system and web server software, many web servers use additional technologies to handle back-end processing before serving a page. These are also called server-side platforms or server-side languages. In August 2024, 76% of servers whose server-side platforms we know were using PHP, 6% were using ASP.NET or Ruby, and 5% were using Java. PHP, Ruby, and Java are all languages, but ASP.NET is a platform that allows code to be written using one of three languages: Visual Basic, C#, or F#.

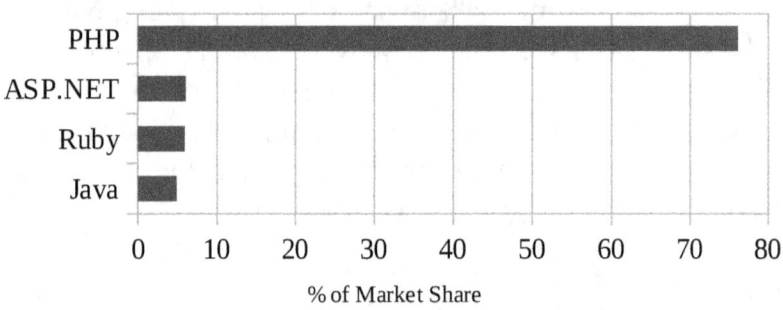

Figure 4.5.3. PHP (hypertext preprocessor) dominates the known server-side scripting languages, followed by Microsoft's ASP.NET. Note that ASP.NET can be coded using a variety of Microsoft-supported languages, including Visual Basic, C#, and F#.

Each of these platforms can stack on a variety of operating systems and web server software. For example, ASP.NET can run on IIS, Nginx, Apache, and more. With the exception of IIS, which is Windows-only, any web server software can support ASP.NET on both Windows and Unix. The same is true of each of the other server-side platforms: Nearly any platform can be stacked on nearly any web server software, which can be stacked on nearly any operating system.

Many web sites add additional layers to their web hosting stack. For example, WordPress is a popular content management system (CMS) that was used on 44% of web sites in August 2024. It usually runs on a stack of Unix, Apache or Nginx, and PHP, with MySQL (My server query language) running as a relational database. WordPress has a commanding portion of the known CMS market share. Shopify is the next largest platform (5% of web sites), followed by Wix (3%), Squarespace (2%), and Joomla (2%).

Approximately 69% of web sites use one or more CMSs.

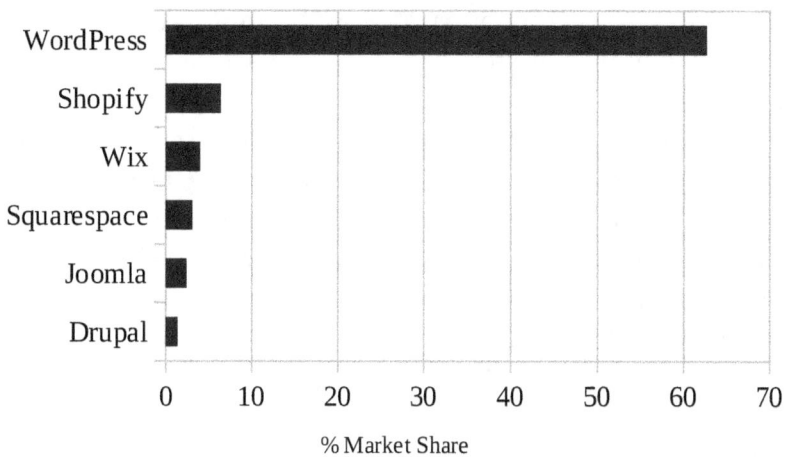

Figure 4.5.4. WordPress greatly outranks all other content management systems. Only 43% of sites use WordPress; however, 63% of sites that use a CMS use WordPress.

Developing for Accessibility
Titles II and III of the Americans with Disabilities Act (ADA) require that governments and public businesses make web sites accessible to people with disabilities. People who have disabilities affecting their fine motor skills may use voice recognition software to navigate their computer. People who are blind may use voice recognition software

and screen readers or refreshable Braille displays to read the text on screen. People who are deaf or hard of hearing may need captioning. People with cognitive disabilities may need text available in an alternative format, such as a video.

Screen readers, voice recognition software, and other tools for navigating a web site rely on the software's ability to understand how web pages are laid out, which elements on the page are interactive, and how to interact with those elements. If the software cannot parse your business's web site, it can be difficult or impossible for people with disabilities to use your site, much like stairs can prevent wheelchair users from entering your building. As more and more business is conducted online, web accessibility only becomes more critical.

A full overview of the techniques required to meet web-based accessibility standards (A11y, as in "a," 11 characters, then "y") is beyond the scope of this text, but it is important to understand how A11y fits into web design. Web accessibility standards are known as the Web Content Accessibility Guidelines (WCAG), published by the non-profit W3C, the World Wide Web Consortium. Version 2.2 of these standards includes multiple success criteria related to 13 guidelines, with each criterion identified as compliance level A (essential), AA (ideal), and AAA (support for specialized audiences). Level A and AA are required by the ADA. WCAG 2.2 guidelines include:

1. Providing alternatives to text;
2. Providing alternatives for time-based media, including captions, audio descriptions, or sign language;
3. Making characteristics such as relationships, sequences, and input purposes computer-readable;
4. Ensuring content is distinguishable from the background, including through the use of contrast

and control of audio;
5. Providing keyboard-based methods to navigate;
6. Managing time-based features, including slowing or stopping moving content and extending authentication timeouts;
7. Minimizing flashes to negate the possibility of seizures or other physical reactions;
8. Providing context for navigation items, including headings, labels, and other descriptions of purpose;
9. Eliminating the need for multiple pointers and responding to mis-clicks with grace;
10. Noting the language of pages or parts of pages and providing alternatives for high-reading-level text;
11. Ensuring all inputs, navigation, and help systems are predictable;
12. Helping users avoid and correct input errors; and
13. Maximizing compatibility with present and future assistive technologies.

There are helpful checklists available, but it is important to think about accessibility well before evaluating your business's web site using an interactive checklist such as the one provided by the A11y Project (https://a11yproject.com/checklist/).

Good, accessible web design starts with using HTML elements as they are intended. For example, headings (e.g., <h1> and <h2>) elements should be used to make web pages navigable to machines. Buttons should be made from a <button> element not images. If unusual acronyms are used, the <abbr> element exists for a reason. Some of these elements are easy to alter in WYSIWYG editors, but even in professional editors, code editing is required for maximum WCAG compliance.

Contrast is important to users with low vision, but it is

helpful to fully sighted users as well: links should always be a different color from surrounding text (links that blend in may seem like a clean design choice, but they are often inaccessible to all users). A volume knob is not a standard HTML element, so if JavaScript and CSS are used to turn a range slider into a knob, the element should be well-labeled and remain accessible to keyboards and other input devices.

After good, accessible web design comes good, accessible web development. Behind the scenes, developers can add extra semantic information that will be invisible to the average user. For example, `<nav>` and `<footer>` HTML elements allow users of screen readers to move throughout the page far more quickly, but these sections do not have to be labeled visually. Alternate text should be added to images, or the browser should be informed that an image is purely decorative (by setting `alt=""`).

When good design and good standard development fail (when complex features and navigation are unavoidable), ARIA (Accessible Rich Internet Applications) is a W3C-provided standard for assigning roles and semantics through HTML properties such as `role="menuitem"` to identify parts of unusual menus or `aria-required="true"` to specify fields that must be completed for a form to validate. ARIA data provides information only; it does not change page behavior. However, ARIA information is something screen readers will dwell upon, so it should only be provided when needed. Including unnecessary information actually makes web pages less accessible.

If you start with good web design, and you follow the KISS (keep it simple…) mantra, accessibility can be relatively easy. However, this chapter began with a description of jobs in web development for good reason—experts in fields such as web accessibility are available for hire to double-check your work. And it is always better to pay a small amount up front than to face a lawsuit over an inaccessible web site.

Resources for Language Learning
If you are an aspiring web developer, what technologies should you learn? Most developers learn the most popular technologies because there are the most jobs available for people with those skill sets. There is also more support available for these most common technologies. This is the path we will take momentarily, but it is worth noting that unpopular technologies have an appeal as well—skills in those areas are harder to find, so the few jobs available may pay a premium.

If you want to train yourself on the most common software stack, the stack of Linux, Nginx, PHP, and MySQL is the clear winner. Managing Linux and Nginx does not require a deep amount of knowledge—just enough to keep packages up to date and to make necessary configuration changes. If you use a GUI (Graphic User Interface) for MySQL, such as phpMyAdmin, your focus can be on the basics of setting up and operating a relational database as well as the steps required to secure that database. Simple web sites will not require an in-depth knowledge of data formats like JSON or server-side languages like PHP, but they are powerful. The more knowledge and experience a developer has with a language, the more efficiently they and the server can work. (Experienced developers can often optimize code by choosing the fastest method to accomplish each task.)

In addition to knowing how to use these back-end technologies, it is important that you are able to work with the front-end languages of HTML, CSS, and JavaScript.

There is no substitute for investing your time in a

project that uses these technologies, but if you were looking to invest your time on a full learning path, you can refer to the following resources.

HTML
- https://www.codecademy.com/learn/learn-html
- https://www.w3schools.com/html/

CSS
- https://www.codecademy.com/learn/learn-css
- https://www.w3schools.com/css/
- https://www.codecademy.com/learn/learn-intermediate-css

JavaScript
- https://www.codecademy.com/learn/introduction-to-javascript
- https://www.w3schools.com/js/
- https://www.codecademy.com/learn/learn-intermediate-javascript

Linux
- https://training.linuxfoundation.org/training/introduction-to-linux/
- https://www.codecademy.com/learn/introduction-to-linux-installation

Nginx
- https://nginx.org/en/docs/beginners_guide.html

PHP
- https://www.learn-php.org/
- https://www.w3schools.com/PHP/php_intro.asp

MySQL
- https://www.codecademy.com/learn/learn-sql
- https://www.khanacademy.org/computing/computer-programming/sql
- https://www.mysqltutorial.org/

W3Schools, Stack Overflow, and MDN (Mozilla Developer Network) can be great general resources as you work through specific tasks or problems.

Libraries and Frameworks
Before you begin your work, it is worth addressing libraries and frameworks. Libraries are collections of related code shortcuts called up on demand to automate a complex task. Like libraries, frameworks provide shortcuts, but they invert the control: They are typically used at all times, so they demand that developers follow the framework's blueprint at all times. With frameworks, there is usually a single best way to accomplish each task.

Libraries such as jQuery and Processing can reduce the amount of work required to accomplish a single task, but especially for beginners, libraries may not have a place in simple projects. Beginning with a framework can be valuable if you know your employer uses one as a standard, but both libraries and frameworks require learning yet another toolset that will invariably slow down the development process.

Libraries and frameworks are much more likely to change over time when compared to true languages, so avoiding libraries and frameworks will often reduce the amount of maintenance required for simple projects. Avoiding libraries offers a benefit for your users as well—until your web site has become complex enough to benefit from the library, you are saving your users from downloading and processing it when they visit your site. To see the impact of libraries (as well as other people- and environment-friendly metrics) on your web site, visit https://ecograder.com/.

Figure 4.5.5 shows the impact of unused JavaScript on the Ecograder score for a single web page. The Web.Dev site includes references to six unused scripts and one unused stylesheet, all associated with Google's Tag Manager library for search engine optimization. If that library was only served to Google robots instead of all visitors and one JPEG file was converted to a space-saving WEBP (with no loss of image quality), the site would have earned 100/100. Users would also be downloading 300kb less content, and load time would be decreased by 110ms.

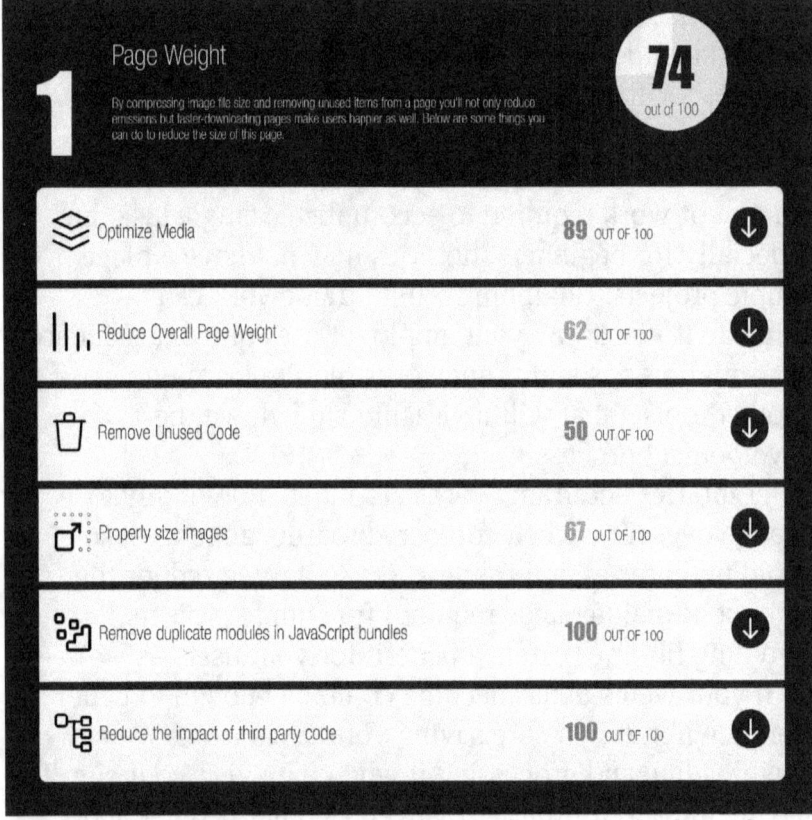

Figure 4.5.5. The Ecograder report for a Web.Dev article shows the impact of extra scripts on a web page's page weight, download time, and associated carbon emissions. The page scored a 50/100 for unused code, 74/100 for page weight, and 80/100 for the overall score.

The formula for business success is a lot like success at a casino. More than mere luck, you must be looking for trends in data. Fortunately, gathering information is much easier on the web than at a roulette wheel.

Section 4.6 Web Analytics

Web analytics is the collection, analysis, and reporting of web site data. Web analytics should lead to continued improvement of your customers' online experience, which should, in turn, translate into the outcomes your business desires.

Although it is possible for directionless data collection to lead to new insights, most successful analytics programs are goal- or objective-driven, with specific qualitative and quantitative data points collected, analyzed, and reported.

Quantitative measurements are those that can be counted or measured in size. Most of the traditional metrics of the web are quantitative, including page views, time spent on a page/site, the number of clicks, or the number of times a user purchases a specific item.

Qualitative measurements cannot be counted or have their size measured directly. Instead, qualitative measures go beyond numbers to describe patterns in data and the meaning those patterns have for people. Qualitative measures may begin as categorical, as in device metrics (e.g., 51% of visitors use mobile devices) or visitor

123

geography (e.g., 10% of visitors come from Swaziland). Qualitative measures may also be more free-form, as in search terms (e.g., 100 visitors arrived after searching for "headphones" versus 76 visitors who searched for "wireless headphones"). Traffic patterns are also free-form in nature, but they can be based on unique data such as mouse action heat maps or be based on combined data such as where customers go from the home page or what users were doing right before they left your site.

    A successful analytics program uses both forms of measurement with deep exploratory analysis and analysis based on a company's objectives. Consider the following objective: *After our team publishes 3 months of posts, 10,000 people will be following our social media.* At a glance, it may seem easy to classify this as requiring simple quantitative analysis. If you add together the followers/subscribers of each social media platform, you've counted the number of people, right? Not really. Although "people" was not explicitly defined in the objective, it would certainly be more meaningful if 10,000 *different* people engaged with your social media. If the platforms allow you to, you might treat your followers categorically, subtracting overlapping usernames or IP addresses or using other methods to identify unique users.

    What if you learned that 50% of your followers had accounts with names/handles comprised of three or four random letters and numbers? That kind of deeper analysis may be suggestive that a large portion of your followers are not real people, a fact verified if these types of usernames often try to post clickbait or other spam to your company's pages.

    If your business is frequently analyzing these kinds of data points, you can quickly respond to any problems or take advantage of any unforeseen opportunities. You would likely want to ensure your true followers are not pushed away by spamming accounts, including the simple response of communicating with your community. Employees, followers, and investors alike—really, all your stakeholders—could find value in those insights by way of an apology (e.g., "We know that spam is becoming a problem within our community. Please know that we are actively engaged in managing this problem with every tool available to us as well as by engaging with platform moderators and management. If your message to us is lost as we address these issues, please reach out to us at...").

It is critical that these analyses take place frequently, both regularly and irregularly. If your company conducts only snapshot analyses (e.g., monthly or quarterly), you are likely to miss out on both threats and opportunities, but setting up a regular reporting schedule can also have value. You can regularly update your stakeholders through public data sharing (e.g., "this quarter, we saw a 10% increase in traffic and a 20% increase in revenue"). The spam example discussed previously would merit an irregular announcement, but increases in traffic, trending product preferences, and more might be shared with social media followers on a more regular schedule.

Analytics in Product Testing

Businesses often use analytics to help them make decisions, big and small.

A/B testing is the easiest form to conduct. For example, will more customers who see a black pair of headphones make a purchase, or will they react better to a red pair of headphones? By showing two different images and tracking the purchases that follow, you may choose to change the default color.

Multivariate testing occurs when more than one change

appears to a single customer. For example, customers may see different colored images, but they may also be shown different default views (e.g., head-on, profile, or isometric). This is an analysis of two variables, but one has three options—your audience will see one of six different images. Multivariate testing requires sufficient traffic and a different type of analysis, but just like A/B testing, it can lead to very successful decision making.

What should you test? We have talked a bit about aesthetics (changes in appearance or "feel"), but we can (and should!) also test navigability. Do customers know where to go and what path(s) lead to the outcomes they (or your company) want? What about functionality? If we give them options, do customers prefer to change their password by e-mail verification or text message? The less friction there is in a user experience, the longer we are likely to keep that user as a customer.

One of the most important areas to test is what returning customers do or encounter that might be different than one-time or no-time customers. One of the highest costs for a business, especially a new business, is the cost of customer acquisition and retention (CAR, discussed in greater depth in *Section 5.2: Advertising Strategies*). If you can learn why customers want to return to your web site, you can more effectively retain those customers and, potentially, reduce the cost of your next sale.

The Internet of Things uses sensors to collect large amounts of data. We can learn new things based on the analysis of that data, such as predicting when equipment might fail. Even large devices benefit from small sensors.

Case Study 4 Industrial Analytics

IoT (internet of things) refers to collections of sensors that can work together to greater effect. General Electric (GE) had used sensors for decades, but only around the year 2010 did GE and several other companies begin to collect, analyze, and apply insights from their sensors. Prior to that time, sensors allowed users to monitor real-time performance (e.g., pressure and temperature), but the data was not collected, only observed by an operator.

By including sensors in their gas turbines, jet engines, and other machines and analyzing the collected data, GE believed its "Industrial Internet" could lead the company to improve machine productivity, efficiency, and reliability. A single unproductive day at a liquefied natural gas (LNG) facility can cost as much as $25 million, so reduced downtime is incredibly valuable to GE's customers. Similarly, the typical oil well extracts only about 35% of the available oil before its operation becomes uneconomical, so even a small improvement in productivity would be incredibly valuable.

Enter Predix, GE's software platform designed to

collect and analyze 50 million data points across 10 million sensors. (This is "big data," data that is complex enough to require new, parallel approaches to data analysis.) The first iteration of the software saved GE's aviation customers an average of $7 million in jet fuel through one simple insight: A failure to clean engines more regularly in hot and harsh environments such as the Middle East was leading to reduced efficiency and frequent jet engine maintenance.

In 2015, GE launched Predix 2.0 as a platform to allow customers to build their own analytics. The oil and gas market was the one most likely to see sizable improvements in productivity, but it was also a market that was historically conservative—few operations would invest in new technology until it was well-proven. As a result, GE needed to identify forward-minded companies that would cooperate in an pilot and serve as an example for others.

GE enlisted RasGas, a LNG plant operator, to install sensors on heat exchangers and valves upstream from the GE equipment to get a broader picture of efficiencies and points of failure.

Although improved efficiency and prevented equipment failures seem like straightforward benefits for the customer, what does GE get? In return for keeping equipment running above an agreed-upon threshold, GE has access to RasGas's data and will receive a bonus payment. Additionally, GE has the benefit of promoting brand loyalty both at RasGas and with similar LNG customers who will hear a new success story.

GE doesn't always have that level of access to data—they work with customers to determine where data will be stored and processed. In some cases, infrastructure is provided by the customer; however, in many cases, Predix uses GE's CDN. In either case, data transactions take place using TLS-encrypted packets over TCP/IP web protocols.

Predix most commonly runs on a stack of Yocto Linux OS, a Nginx web server, and additional layers of customized GE software. The web servers that store the data are set up to manage data access, backups/redundancy, and other factors related to security and reliability.

Beyond infrastructure, the design is modular: Customers are able to drag and drop different metrics in GE's CMS to get the best view of their equipment and business metrics. The metrics may be standard to the software (e.g., GE-developed equipment uptime metrics) or they may have been developed by the customer. As shown in *Figure CS4.1*, the main menu is iconified with additional navigation along the top of the screen: by topic (tabs) and by time (the drop-down list).

Figure CS4.1. GE's Predix software showing key performance indicators (KPIs) such as equipment availability, downtime, and mean time between failures.

Teams at GE developed the initial design, but it has been refined during and following pilot tests with customers.

Predix has proven to be a success story for GE and its customers: 3–40% reductions in environmental health and safety incidents, 2–6% increased equipment availability, 10–40% less reactive maintenance, a 5–10% inventory cost reduction, a 5–35% gain in employee productivity, and a 5–25% reduction in IT total cost of ownership.

Some of this progress may be a result of GE's presence in the Digital Twin Consortium, which aims to leverage analytics technology to simulate a customer's equipment in its current condition. Through the digital twin application, customers can predict what would happen to efficiency if a part were replaced sooner or later or what the economic impacts might be of increasing or decreasing the pressure of gas in a natural gas pipeline.

Questions to Consider
1. What are the advantages and disadvantages of making industrial equipment sensor data available through the Internet?
2. Why would GE have likely chosen Linux as the hosting and development platform for Predix?
3. From a user interface perspective, how could the Predix software be improved? What changes would you make to the menu, navigation, filters, or on-screen data to make it best for the majority of users?
4. Part of the Predix platform is a CMS. How can a CMS such as Predix lead to more or less accessibility for end users who use assistive technology?
5. Predix is a platform built on analytics. How do you think analytics was used to capture early user experiences and improve the features, navigation, and design of the platform?

Chapter 5.0 **Communicating with Stakeholders**

If you have carefully considered the user interface and user experience in designing and developing your web site, that is an advantage, but your web site may not be the first or only impression stakeholders will get of your business. Customers may first encounter an advertisement or social media post. Employees may see a job posting or a social media post. Investors may see your business mentioned in the news or first encounter your business as a customer.

Can you control the first impression of these many disparate parties? If you could, how would you want to shape that first impression?

Furthermore, how can you shape later impressions and help your stakeholders repeatedly engage with your business? How close can you get to two-way communication between an individual customer and your business?

To answer these questions, we will take a closer look at marketing: the processes and analyses involved in producing, promoting, and distributing products. Managers use marketing when they consider inputs, transformations, and outputs through an analysis of the marketing mix: product, price, promotion, and place.

By making strategic marketing plans, especially with the help of customer relationship management tools, you can balance the interests of all stakeholders and ensure long-term business success.

Successful marketing requires a careful and considered approach to the way your company contributes to your products' value chains. Each choice your company makes will strengthen or weaken what you can provide.

Section 5.1 Marketing Strategies

What can you do to ensure that customers engage with your products in the right way, at the right time, and in the right place? The number of processes and analyses involved in producing, placing, promoting, and pricing your products is likely numerous, which means there are many ways your business will contribute to your own revenue and your customers' loyalty.

We have already explored a number of areas that contribute to successful marketing, including a meaningful corporate mission or vision, a thoughtful approach to your competition, and a careful analysis of your stakeholders' needs. (For more information on these topics, see *Section 2.4*, *Section 2.5*, and all of Chapter 3, especially *Section 3.2*.) None of these areas work in isolation, however. Marketing strategy includes strategies for each of the components in the marketing mix: product, place (distribution), promotion, and pricing. Most importantly, marketing strategy looks at how these strategies work together.

Product Strategies
We have already explored how to develop a valuable product offering, but there is more to a product than the offering itself.

With physical goods, marketers will carefully develop physical packaging, and the same is true of virtual goods—the way an app is presented on a web store may influence a customer's decisions. Colors, fonts, logos, and imagery are visual elements a marketer can control, but there are also textual elements. What tag lines can you use to attract attention? What truthful claims can you make about your product? What product information can be placed on packaging to answer customer questions before they are asked?

A product can also include other forms of added value. Service after the sale (through a warranty or other program) can be valuable to the customer and can influence whether or not they will be a returning customer. Similarly, free updates to software or data can add value. Even a good recommendation algorithm can bring customers back to an otherwise so-so service.

Place Strategies
How are you going to distribute your products? If you look back at *Section 2.5: Conducting Market Research*, you will notice that headphones were identified as being sold direct or through Amazon, Best Buy, Crutchfield, or Walmart. Each of these is a different distribution channel that offers unique advantages.

Direct sales may be the most important because only your own web site or storefront gives you full control over what customers see about the product at its point of sale.

Other types of distributors may offer their own advantages, however. A key advantage is access to a bigger pool of customers. Amazon offers hundreds of millions of products, so it has a high level of competition, but its nearly 200 million unique monthly U.S. users are an appealing customer pool.

The reputation of a place can be important too. Best Buy is a place where people often go to try out new technology, so it is a great place for a product like headphones. Crutchfield is a retailer known for premium sound products, so audiophiles may go there first.

Finally, general retailers such as Walmart offer the dual advantages of large reach and a fairly small number of products per category. If our headphones were stocked at Walmarts across the country, we would be virtually guaranteed sales.

Promotional Strategies
There are three main forms of communication with customers or potential customers. When you think about marketing, you likely think first about mass communication through modes such as advertising. Regardless of the medium (print, radio, e-mail, social media, etc.), mass communication requires a marketer to choose a target market segment to concentrate on (see *Section 2.3: Identifying Target Markets* for more about market segmentation). Additional audiences will see the message; however, for all but a few well-established consumer product brands, targeted advertising has proven to be more effective than a general or "shotgun" approach.

In addition to mass communication, there are two forms of interpersonal communication. In the first form, the customer is communicating with your company, usually through sales, support, or other public relations teams. These direct interpersonal communications, especially if initiated by the customer, are incredibly valuable opportunities to ensure the customer feels heard and helped. Happy customers are return customers, and they will likely be peer marketers or informal "brand ambassadors."

Peer marketing is the second form of interpersonal marketing. Your business may be able to shape customer-to-customer interactions, but in many cases, your business will have no control over these exchanges. (See *Section 5.3: Social Media* for ideas on how to increase the chances of positive social media interactions.)

Whatever the form or mode of communication, it is important to remember that promotional activities involve two independent processes: sending and receiving. The message you send may not always be received and understood in the way that you intend. It is important to have a diverse marketing staff and to have all eyes on all campaigns. Major promotional campaigns should be tested with focus groups to ensure the messaging is clear and not offensive—offending even a small group of customers can be detrimental. If you are including coupons or other discounts in the promotion, focus groups can give you a much better read on perceived value than your own staff.

Finally, it is important to note that the advertising approach can have an impact on how ads are received by consumers. When a brand needs to overcome negative opinions, serious or dramatic ads are best. When a brand already has a good reputation, humor can help your ads maintain positivity.

Price Strategies
Price is the final factor to consider when developing a marketing strategy. Prices are likely to change throughout the life of a product. The Product Life Cycle is described below a typical product sales curve in *Figure 5.1.1*.

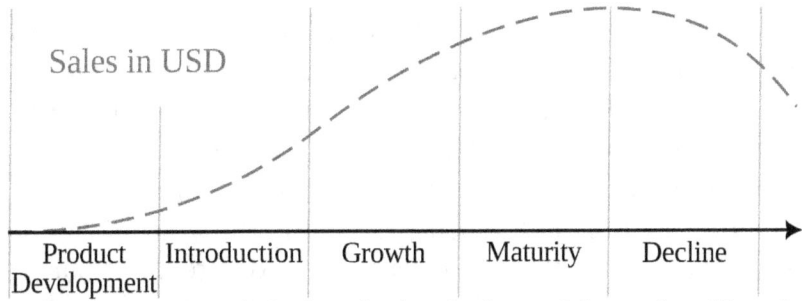

Figure 5.1.1. Although the length of each phase of the product lifecycle can vary, sales typically follow the illustrated path. Sales inch up during a period of product development and then slowly increase during a period of introduction. Sales quickly accelerate during a period of growth, accelerate more slowly during a period of maturity, and gradually decrease during a period of decline.

During a period of product development, there may be no (or few) sales. Early adopters will be the main audience during the introduction phase, and a period of sales growth will usually follow. When a product reaches maturity, its sales will begin to level out, to be followed by a period of decline as a product is no longer needed or as a better product emerges.

The initial sales price often depends on the expected audience of the product. For consumable or subscription-based products, initial prices are often based on penetration pricing—the product is priced lower than competitors to capture a larger portion of the market more quickly. If the product serves a premium market, prices are often priced above competitors (to denote uniqueness and capture profit in a method called price skimming). If your product is non-consumable, and your company prices a product near its competitors, it is called status quo pricing.

Of course, pricing based on competitors' prices is a luxury not all companies will have. The more important marketing consideration is whether you can produce your product (and pay for overhead as well as repay development costs) at a given price point. In order to determine pricing, a company should complete a draft of its financial projections early in the product development process (see *Chapter 6: Business Finances*). Product, place, and promotional changes can all impact pricing decisions, but you need to know early in the process if you will need to reduce your product feature set in order to make it at the expected cost. Only by repeatedly evaluating the whole marketing mix can we hope to meet our business objectives.

Revisiting Objectives
When you begin to put product, place, promotion, and price together, it is a good idea to revisit your business's measurable objectives, both to make sure you are on track and to add/revise objectives as necessary.

Customer-focused objectives often have overlapping goals of informing, persuading, reminding, and connecting. For example, an objective might be for 90% of customers to be using the latest active noise cancellation firmware in their headphones. This is an appealing goal because customers will get the best experience when they are running the best software, and they will feel more connected with the product and the company. The first communications on the subject of ANC will inform customers that an update is available with later communications reminding them to update. Some customers may eventually need persuasion in order to meet the objective, but persuasion is often difficult to achieve; if a potential customer needs to be persuaded, your efforts may be better exerted finding more engaged, new customers.

Revisiting your objectives will be a key consideration when you put together the marketing plan we will discuss in *Section 5.5: Marketing Plans*.

Times Square in New York City is well-lit, overwhelming, and representative of the chaos that can come from seeking to stand out.

Section 5.2 Advertising Strategies

Advertising is an extension of promotion. Although promotion includes a wider variety of customer interactions, advertising focuses on impersonal, paid promotions in which the sponsor company is identified. Unlike most promotional strategies, advertising is largely unidirectional. It is this advertiser-to-customer limitation that makes advertising strategy worthy of a section of its own.

Achieving success through advertising often requires the customer to move through four stages referred to as the AIDA model: attention, interest, desire, and action.

Figure 5.2.1 shows part of a 2006 LifeLock campaign that used CEO Todd Davis's confidence in the company's service to encourage customers to subscribe to its identity protection service. There is no doubt that the advertising campaign attracted attention: Davis published his Social Security Number and declared, "No, I'm not crazy. I'm just sure our system works." The $10 monthly price of LifeLock's service, combined with their "$1 million guarantee," also gained potential customers' interest. For potential customers who had experienced identity theft, the difficult memory of clearing their name and credit report

139

instilled a desire to take action and subscribe to the service.

Figure 5.2.1. Todd Davis, then CEO of LifeLock, portrayed confidence in his company's service in an advertising campaign that publicized his social security number.

Especially with new products, helping a customer to move through the stages of AIDA can increase the chances they will achieve the final action. Unfortunately, the effectiveness of LifeLock's advertising campaign invited scrutiny, and investigators found that, despite the LifeLock service, Davis's identity was stolen at least 13 times. The company had to pay a $12 million false advertising fine to the U.S. Federal Trade Commission (FTC) and settled a related FTC enforcement action for $100 million.

Whether your company seeks to inform, persuade, remind, or connect with customers, your company needs to think through all the consequences (positive and negative) before embarking on an advertising campaign.

Ad development generally begins with the attention stage of AIDA. Ads can appeal to the attention of consumers in one of eight ways, promoting: admiration, conscientiousness, convenience, fear, fun/pleasure, health, profit, and/or vanity/egotism. The LifeLock campaign offered customers convenience and a path to allaying fear. LADbible's 2018 "Trash Isles" campaign offered customers a taste of admiration, environmental conscientiousness, and fun when it rallied subscribers to support their proposal to turn the France-sized "Great Pacific Garbage Patch" into a new country named "Trash Isle" as a means of recruiting the United Nations (UN) to help clean it up. Anne Arundel's Medical Center promoted health through egotism with a "Stachie" contest on Facebook, asking customers to share selfies with 'staches (in a branded photo frame) to raise awareness for men's health.

Generating attention and interest is an important goal—only through those stages can a company hope to earn customer desire or action. Because only a fraction of customers will move between stages, a high number of customers must be engaged in the attention stage.

Digital advertising can be a powerful way to move customers who may already have interest into the desire or action stages: digital advertising often permits the advertiser to communicate with a target market segment that meets behavioral, demographic, geographic, or psychographic criteria (see *Section 2.3: Identifying Target Markets*).

Many companies are competing for the same customers' attention and wallets. Cutting through the array of messages presented to customers every day requires many impressions plus enough advertising data to target a receptive audience. Of course, a well-crafted message matters as well! Consider the variety of executional styles:

- **Demonstration:** By showing a product in use, potential customers are more likely to see the direct benefits they can expect to see from the product.

- **Fantasy:** By depicting a fantastic non-reality, potential customers are more likely to extend their imagination to how the product could benefit their own life.
- **Humor:** By utilizing humor, potential customers are more likely to recall a brand's existing good reputation when considering a product in that brand's category.
- **Lifestyle:** By depicting people experiencing a lifestyle change, potential customers are more likely to see the impact a product could have on their own lives.
- **Mood:** By creating a mood (e.g., love or beauty), potential customers are more likely to remember a brand or product.
- **Musical:** By integrating music, potential customers are more likely to remember a brand or product.
- **Scientific:** By using scientific evidence, potential customers are more likely to believe in one brand's superiority over another.
- **Slice-of-Life:** By depicting people living a typical life, potential customers are more likely to relate to the situation in the ad.
- **Testimonial:** By speaking directly to the consumer (especially if the testimonial comes from a respected celebrity), potential customers are more likely to see the ad as truthful.

Many of these executional styles emphasize the idea of "selling the sizzle, not the steak," or focusing on the benefits the product can bring, not on the product itself.

Customer Acquisition and Retention

Customer acquisition and retention (CAR) is tracked through customer acquisition costs, customer retention rate, and customer churn. Each of these metrics is easy to calculate, for example, customer acquisition costs (CAC) compares the number of new customers to the total marketing costs for that period of time. Each of these metrics is also incredibly important. E-businesses will commonly spend $70 to acquire each new customer.

This may seem like a lot, but you cannot judge CAC by itself; a good CAC is determined in comparison with a customer's lifetime value (LTV). Average CAC should be a third or less of a customer's average LTV. If you spend $70 per new customer, your business needs to make an average of $210 or more per customer.

How much should you spend? Digital advertising tends to have a low cost per contact, but like traditional advertising, the total cost is still high. According to an analysis of Google AdWords campaigns in March 2024, the average cost per click (CPC) across all industries is $4.66. At an average conversion rate of 6.7%, it costs a business an average of $66.69 in online ads to turn ad impressions into a new customer. Social media advertising tends to cost a bit less. Using Facebook as an example, the average CPC was $1.92 in 2023, with an average conversion rate of 8.25% and a cost per lead of $23.10. Why the difference? Most experts attribute the higher conversion rate to the attention or interest gathered by the graphics in social media ads and the lower CPC to reduced ad supply in a medium where creating and targeting ads can be very energy intensive.

Practical Advertising Advice

We will end this section with a discussion of some practical tips for potential advertisers, but as with legal and financial matters, it is always best to consult with an expert. Advertising firms specialize in navigating constantly changing customer trends, so setting aside part of your advertising budget for a skilled consultant will often pay off.

1. **Attention and interest lead to desire and action.** It is easy to focus on the result you seek from advertising, but the best campaigns focus first on attention and interest, then on desire and action goals.
2. **Think through consequences (both positive and negative).** What do you hope your campaign will achieve? What could happen to prevent success? Don't forget that your full staff and focus groups can help you prevent miscommunications by providing feedback when your campaign is still in draft mode.
3. **Consider target market, advertising medium, and time.** Although people outside your target market are likely to see your ad, it is always best to create an ad for the audience who is most likely to help you achieve your company's goals. Think as well about where and when your target market is most likely to see your message.
4. **Be prepared to respond to analytics.** Think about what you will be looking for in your ad metrics and how you can pivot if needed. How many people do you want to see your ads? Is your market segmentation working? Be prepared to change content or move between market segments soon after your campaign launches.
5. **Invest in the destination.** Most campaigns will direct traffic to your corporate web site. Be sure to invest time and energy into your site. Keep your web site simple, and avoid pop-ups or animations that might drive customers away.
6. **Be patient.** The first wave of any advertising campaign is unlikely to be perfect, but if you revise your approach in response to analytics, it should improve.

Nearly 75% of American adults use social media, and the majority log on daily. Social media can offer a convenient channel for communication, but viral content can be incredibly helpful or incredibly harmful.

Section 5.3 Social Media

Social media can be an incredible tool for marketers. It offers four unique types of activities: fan acquisition, consumer engagement, network amplification, and community development. Fan acquisition is often the first task your business will engage in—only after customers have self-identified as fans can you begin to engage them in meaningful interactions. As your list of followers grows, customer engagement will lead to network amplification—more friends of followers seeing your content. As your list of followers grows further, you can begin to develop a community—engaging followers in more meaningful activities and replacing some of the content produced by your company with customer-generated content.

Of course, content originating from customers carries risk as well as reward. See the list of pros and cons in *Table 5.3.1* below. To make the most of social media, embrace what makes social media unique: make your social media posts interactive. Asking a question or otherwise including a call to action will directly engage the follower and spread your message more widely.

145

Social Media / Social Advertising	
Pros	Cons
Large Audience • Many people participate in social media, with many participating simultaneously on multiple platforms. • The more people see your brand, the more likely they are to remember it and try your product.	*Time Consuming* • Engaging busy Internet denizens requires a great investment in what may ultimately be visible for a number of hours at most. • Preparing messages for traditional media is more time-intensive, but longer lasting.
Interactive • Word-of-mouth advertising has always been powerful, and the interactive nature of social ads leverages this power. • Whether you like a company or not, you will likely be shown ads for companies friends like.	*Loss of Control* • The interactive nature of social media necessitates a loss of control—strings of comments can go in any direction. • Unofficial pages often outnumber official ones both in page count and users.
Customer Service • The more easily customers can communicate with you, the more easily customer concerns can be resolved.	*Negative Users* • Publicly aired complaints can quickly go viral, which means social media can be as detrimental as it is helpful.
Brand Loyalty • Brand loyalty is very easy to promote online, and reaching loyal fans to notify them of new products and services has never been easier.	*Diluted Voice* • Without a carefully controlled strategy and in-sync social marketing staff, messages can lose the voices of your company as phrasing and tone shift.
Low Cost • Social ads, whose prices are usually based on impressions or clicks, usually cost much less (and can be much more specifically targeted) than traditional ads.	*Uncertain Return on Investment* • Although tracking the number of viewers and their actions is easy, matching viewers to purchase is not as easy. How can you know if social investment is worth it?

Table 5.3.1. A descriptive list of pros and cons for social media or social media advertising.

To make the most of social media, you can also use social media tools to communicate slightly different versions of the same marketing materials to different market segments. For example, social media platforms make it easy to promote Spanish-language content to Spanish-speaking customers.

If you do encounter friction with social media users, engage with negative users only when there is space to be helpful. Responding to a post that simply states, "I hate your company" only serves to bring the comment to the attention of others. Save your efforts for customers who have specific complaints that you can correct after the fact or that you can use to inform future business decisions.

Returns from Social Media Engagement

Return on Investment (ROI) is a business term typically used to describe a business's profitability. ROI is determined by dividing the net profit by total assets. Most industries achieve around a 10% ROI, though in a hyper-competitive industry such as groceries, less than 5% ROI is normal. When it comes to marketing, the return on a business's marketing investment can be figured by dividing the profit generated by a marketing campaign by the cost of that campaign. Although it is easy to imagine how powerful this knowledge would be, it is often difficult to capture the data required to truly understand a campaign's ROI.

Just wait...RoR (which is arguably a more important metric in the world of social media) is often impossible to quantify! Ted Rubin, who trademarked the phrase, describes it below:

> "RoR (Return on Relationship) is the value accrued by a person or a brand due to nurturing a relationship. ROI (Return on Investment) is simple dollars and cents. RoR is the value (perceived and

real) that will accrue over time through loyalty, recommendations, and sharing."

Fortunately, you do not need to calculate RoR to pursue an enriching relationship with customers. Instead, you simply need to follow a few key steps.

1. **Listen to your customers.** What are they saying and feeling? If you can understand problems from their perspective, you can develop solutions that work for them and ensure a long and fruitful relationship.
2. **Make everything you do about the customer.** If you make what matters most to the customer matter most to you, you can ensure the customer will be well served and will more likely be loyal.
3. **Broadcast your willingness to serve customers.** Marketing is far more than advertising; it is a chance to build a relationship. If customers hear "How can I serve you?" as your primary message, they will be more willing to listen to your response.
4. **Aim for ongoing engagement.** The most meaningful relationships are long-lasting, with two-way communication playing a key part in keeping customers engaged. Customers may be interested in your updates, but they are more likely to be interested in contributing to a more perfect solution to the problem your product solves.

Don't forget that your audience is made of people. Businesses often focus on money, but people are more than mere sources of funding. If you have to think about money, think about the money a deeper relationship can make you now and into the future.

No matter what form your business takes, the customer comes first. If you listen to your customers, even in the form of anonymous web analytics data, you can better serve customers, and they may become loyal to you.

Section 5.4 Customer Relationship Management

Customer Relationship Management (CRM) is a cornerstone of modern e-commerce. If your business actively engages in CRM, you are working to address customer needs through relationships at both large and small scales with long-term profitability and survival in mind.

The following steps are key considerations for the successful implementation of CRM:
1. identifying individual customers and how they can best be reached,
2. segmenting customers by needs and values,
3. using segmentation to engage individual customers in dialogue customized to them (through personal contact or automation), and
4. listening to customers' changing needs and responding to them.

<u>Stages of the Customer Life Cycle</u>
With appropriate CRM, customers can be ushered through the different stages of the customer life cycle. This is not a passive process. Customers respond to business behaviors as

they move closer to or away from a commitment to your business.

The first stage of the customer life cycle is awareness. Customers can encounter your business in many ways, but, ideally, this first contact will occur as part of a coordinated marketing strategy and marketing plan (see *Section 5.5: Marketing Plans*). In this stage, you should begin populating your CRM system with customer data such as referral source and click path—that data may prove critical in the next stage.

The next stage of the customer life cycle is exploration. Customers will be collecting information about your offerings and deciding whether or not your offerings best meet their needs. It is at this stage that CRM software is most critical. If you can use an automated system to understand customer needs, provide access to the right information, and, perhaps, give customers a reason to complete their first few sales, you will help them move to the third stage.

After exploration comes familiarity. After a few successful transactions, your customer may become comfortable with your business and consider your offerings when they have a need. This stage is also aided by a CRM system for the same reasons as the exploration stage. Of course, knowing what customers actually buy is far more valuable than knowing what customers are looking at. In the familiarity stage, your CRM system can help you reach out to customers for follow-up after the sale.

Commitment is the ideal stage—customers have graduated beyond considering your business to preferring your company. When customers have this brand loyalty, it should be maintained through follow-up communications and promotions. These customers can become brand advocates, so you can consider using your CRM software to set up a referral program. With referral programs, you can reward your existing customers and sweeten the deal for new customers.

The final stage marks the end of the stages of customer loyalty: separation. When customers become disappointed, disenchanted, or find a better option, they may move away from your company. With CRM, you may be able to preempt this stage by pivoting to meet customers' new needs, resolving customers' problems, or otherwise working to maintain customer loyalty.

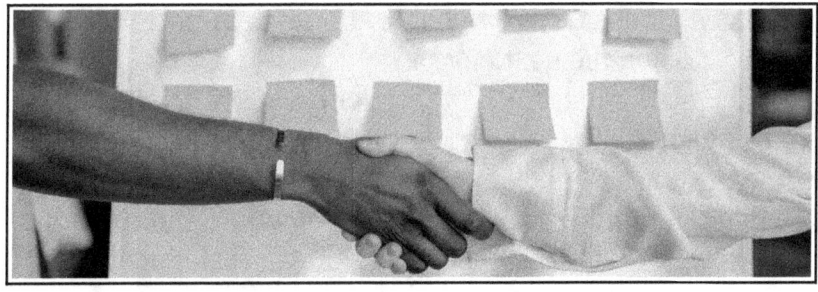

Marketing plans require agreement within teams and between your company, suppliers, distributors, customers and more. A good marketing plan starts with a good marketing team who knows these stakeholders well.

Section 5.5 Marketing Plans

Every marketing decision serves as a communication to your stakeholders. Even if it does not affect your customers, each marketing choice will affect employees, suppliers, investors, or perhaps even competitors.

A marketing plan is designed to give internal stakeholders (employees and investors) a view of the company or group's marketing activities. A plan may be created at different time scales: sometimes weekly but generally monthly or quarterly. If the marketing plan is presented as a table, time is usually identified in each column. Rows will include the business directive, marketing strategy, objectives, marketing campaigns, and always-on marketing.

The business directive is a very high-level overview of the marketing goal for that time period, often related to launching a new product, a support service, or a new opportunity for customer interactions. For example, one quarter's business directive may be to build a social media following, whereas the next may be to gather customer feedback through focus groups. (These directives are presented alongside additional detail in the sample plan, *Table 5.5.1*, on the next page.)

The marketing strategy description offers details related to the business directive, bridging it and the objectives that come next. Marketing strategy often focuses on elements of the marketing mix: product, price, promotion, and place. If the business directive concerns building a social media following, the marketing strategy might describe connections to promotion: developing interest in the product. If the business directive were to gather consumer feedback, the corresponding marketing strategy might describe how the product could be improved through focus-group prototype testing.

The objectives or KPI (key performance indicators), describe how the strategy will be measured. (For more on objectives, see *Section 3.2: Pre- and Post-Investor Analyses*). Although the responsible team(s) within the company may not always be made explicit in objectives, assignments of responsibility should be clear. For example, in "After a series of product development revisions in Q2, focus groups will have awarded a 90%+ satisfaction rating to prototypes of Model 1 & Model 1 Pro at price points of $99 and $199," the product development team is given responsibility for revising the product between focus-group sessions.

Marketing campaigns may have several rows with different campaigns happening in each period of time and with some campaigns continuing across periods. It is most important for marketing campaigns to describe what will be done. If the connection to the business direction is unclear, that should be stated clearly as well. For example, in "Introduce the design team, humanizing the people behind the product," the relevance of the proposed content may be unclear without the added statement about humanization.

	Q1	Q2
Business Directive	Build a social media following.	Gather customers' product feedback.
Marketing Strategy	Develop interest in the product based on its attributes. Use social media responses to each attribute to guide early product design.	The perfect alignment of product, promotion, place, and price can be identified through in-person, focus-group product testing.
Objective / KPI (Key Performance Indicator)	After the marketing team has published content for a quarter[C], 10,000[D] people[A] will be following our social media properties at Facebook, Instagram, and X[B].	After a series of product revisions in Q2[C], focus groups[A] will have awarded[B] a 90%+[D] satisfaction rating to prototypes of Model 1 & Model 1 Pro at price points of $99 and $199.
Marketing Campaigns	Announce product goals: functionality, sustainability, not-for-profit approach.	Schedule biweekly focus-group tests. If the objective is unmet after four sessions, schedule future tests weekly.
	Introduce the design team, humanizing the people behind the product.	Between each test, refine product and promotional packaging design and produce a new set of prototype devices.
	Announce product improvements, supply chain development, and anticipated release dates.	
Always-On Marketing	Respond promptly to customer questions through social media and the web, working to ensure all public interactions are positive ones.	

Table 5.5.1. A short-form marketing plan shows two quarters of activities. Superscripts reference audience, behavior, condition, and degree, as outlined in Section 3.2: Pre- and Post-Investor Analyses.

Always-on marketing describes the things the team will always be doing to support customers, regardless of the specific objectives for that time frame.

A marketing plan is designed to give internal stakeholders a view of the company or group's marketing activities. Its activities will not usually correspond directly with the more detailed activities listed in a daily or weekly Gantt chart (i.e., a bar chart showing a project schedule), but a marketing plan should provide guidance to each of the teams involved in the company's marketing efforts over that period.

Social media, psychology, and a century-old company combined to create a craze to spread hydration, sustainability, and a bit of chaos.

Case Study 5 Viral Marketing

Stanley's Adventure Quencher Tumbler had been discontinued in 2019 when the century-old company found itself reviving the model for a broad new audience. The cup itself holds 40 fluid ounces, hot or cold, and it comes with a lid and a removable straw. It has a tapered shape to fit into cup holders, and it sells for $40–45 retail.

Before 2020, the Stanley tumbler had not been marketed to a specific audience, but when three women from The Buy Guide blog and Instagram account contacted Stanley with a plan to market the product to other women, Stanley agreed to produce 5,000 tumblers for them.

Following posts by The Buy Guide and other influencers, that batch of tumblers sold out in 5 days. Fast-forward 3 years, and the tumblers are still difficult to keep in stock, especially in limited edition colors and prints produced in collaboration with partners such as Starbucks and the Magnolia Network.

The Stanley Tumbler was not the first reusable water bottle to benefit from a fad. In the first part of the 21st century, Nalgene's plastic bottles were favored for their indestructibility. Hydro Flask was a reusable aluminum bottle that became popular in the 2010s, first with an outdoorsy crowd and later with Gen Zers and VSCO girls. Hydro Flasks became a popular item with teens for lots of reasons: teens' interest in environmentalism, the bottles' visibility on social media, and thoughtful product design. Like the Stanley Quencher, Hydro Flasks have a wide mouth (perfect for ice), and they are large enough to be carried rather than tucked into a bag. (A great way for your product to be seen is for it to be out in the open at all times!)

For the Stanley Quencher, the advertising strategy was relatively straightforward: let women tell other women about a great product. According to Griffin Wynne of the Huffington Post, the product "become synonymous with key social demographics, namely Utah moms, beautiful people in athleisure with perfect 'no makeup' makeup and chunky gold jewelry and aspiring influencers who post stylized videos of all the items they own."

Stanley quickly used the increased demand to do a full marketing review: The product became available in trendier colors, they were shipped in greater numbers to Target stores than camping stores, and the price was set for the tumbler to be an affordable luxury item. Despite little traditional advertising, *Figure CS5.1* shows Stanley's success at using deceptively simple photos to promote their products.

Figure CS5.1. Photos of Stanley x Target product lines show how simple photography can communicate who a product is for: the yoga crowd and those pursuing country living.

Stanley's promotional work has been in managing influencers (and their popularity in general) rather than engaging in traditional advertising. Not all interactions on social media have been positive, and Stanley has to carefully consider when to respond to negative press and when to let it pass by. For a product that is intended to be reusable drinkware, there are a surprising number of people collecting the tumblers for a place on a shelf. By making collectible colors and patterns, Stanley feeds into the fad at least as much as they promote sustainability. Of course, they are also keeping consumers engaged—something that is difficult to do for a producer of products intended to last a lifetime.

In November 2023, Stanley had a unique opportunity to leverage positive attention on social media. The car of TikTok user @danimarielttering caught on fire, but the Stanley tumbler seemingly survived unscathed (and with ice in it). To be both empathetic and to highlight the durability of its product, Stanley's president offered to replace the woman's car. As a result, an already-viral video spread further and faster. #StanleyTumbler has over 1 billion views on TikTok and the company's revenue rose tenfold to $750 million in 2023.

Questions to Consider
1. How did Stanley use each component of the marketing mix to revise their approach to marketing the Adventure Quencher?
2. What kinds of objectives do think Stanley had in 2019? In 2023? Today? What kind of events would have led Stanley to rapidly revise its KPIs?
3. Although Stanley offers direct-to-consumer sales, most of their sales happen through retail outlets where they are unable to collect meaningful data on

which consumers they are selling to. How could Stanley be using social media engagement to collect this information?
4. In lieu of developing a Customer Relationship Management solution for consumers, Stanley is likely using CRM software to manage their relationship with resellers. What evidence is there for how well their reseller relationship management is going?
5. Short of selling the same products in new colors, how can Stanley work to keep customers in a familiarity or commitment stage rather than separation? How would these potential actions fit into a traditional marketing plan?

Chapter 6.0 **Business Finances**

Even if you aren't planning to start your business right away, it is important to consider business decisions in light of business finances. Every decision you make is likely a marketing decision: a strategic decision that balances the interests of all your stakeholders. As marketers, we recognize that the value of our product changes across different markets. Water is most valuable to thirsty people in the middle of nowhere; people are more likely to be willing to pay more for water there, but it will also likely cost you more to get it there.

Effective marketing uses variations on the corporate message to reach different audiences. The components of the marketing mix (product, placement, promotion, and price) will look different in the desert than elsewhere. Chilled water may sell better than warm water in a city, but in the desert, temperature may be irrelevant. A vending machine may seem like an oasis in the desert, but vending machines are often ignored in cities. In the desert, "quench your thirst" may be enough of a promotion, but in a city, you may need to promote your water's origin story: "fresh from a natural spring." In every case, price will be a consequence of supply costs and consumer demand as well as what customers are willing to pay.

You may have a price in mind before you have finalized your product, placement, or promotion, but it is essential to reconsider price regularly. As once-hidden expenses come to light, you must determine how your business will remain profitable. In balancing finances, price is a powerful lever!

Throughout this chapter, we will reference the financial projections template for small businesses through SCORE, a resource partner of the U.S. Small Business Administration.

What does your physical location need before the first employee walks in? Start-ups cannot always match the pay of larger competitors, so start-up owners are known for bringing fun, like an in-office rec room.

Section 6.1 Start-Up Expenses

Every business faces expenses even before products are launched, doors are open, or the first customer is served.

After the first few fields on the Directions sheet (company name and starting date), SCORE's Financial Projections Spreadsheet lists different types of start-up revenue and expenses. Fixed assets and operating capital describe expenses, and funding must be sourced to cover the cost of these expenses.

Fixed Assets
Land and buildings are necessary expenses if your business plans to own its own location. These can be estimated by performing a quick search of real-estate listings in your area. For guidance, you can calculate the square footage you need by multiplying the number of employees by 175 square feet and adding the footprint of warehouse shelves, retail space, or equipment. If you will have multiple properties, it is best practice to enter data into these cells using formulas (e.g., =150000+250000 to buy buildings at two sites) and to make notes off to the side (e.g., branch office @ 1501 Sheridan,

main office @ 121 E Main). This allows you to quickly identify where each number came from in the event you or a potential investor have a question.

Equipment will vary depending on your industry, but a quick search can give you fair estimates of equipment costs. Just be sure to consider manufacturing or servicing volumes to ensure you have enough equipment. If a machine can output 5 units per minute, and you intend to sell 200,000 units in a month, you would need to run (and staff) the machine 24 hours a day with no downtime. In the real world, machines run only during staff shifts. Downtime of 5% to 20% is required for repair, preventative maintenance, and to change products on the line.

Furniture and fixtures can often be guesstimated. Do you need $1,000, $2,000, $10,000, or more to furnish your space? Keep in mind that a standard office desk and chair can cost $600–$1500. Doubling that cost for an office space will cover most other furniture and fixtures.

The need for vehicles is likely to depend on your industry, but many service and manufacturing businesses do need to budget for vans or trucks. As with real estate, a quick web search will reveal the cost of local vans or trucks for sale. Used vehicles are cheaper to acquire, though they generally require higher maintenance costs.

Operating Capital

Setting up a retail store, developing a web site, and even tasks like finding suppliers or calculating prices and profit will require employees to begin work before your business serves the public. It is easiest to calculate start-up pay by considering annual salaries. For example, a full-time employee earning a $15 hourly wage will earn approximately $30,000 a year. How many months will they work before your business opens? Remember to use formulas to track your calculations (e.g., =30000/12*2*4 shows four employees working 2 months).

Inventory is important for retail stores and manufacturers of physical goods. Inventory prices should be estimated using costs (e.g., =10*20*5*50 represents 20 shirts in five sizes and 50 styles at $10 each). Note that inventory prices should be wholesale prices, which are commonly 50% or less of retail prices.

Every business will need to pay legal and accounting fees, even if only for setting up the business and producing annual reports. CPAs (certified public accountants) and legal experts have costs ranging from $150 to $500 hourly. Where your costs fall within these ranges depends on your location and the level of expertise needed for the task at hand, but $250 is a fair estimate for either profession. You should account for 4 hours of professional support to start up the simplest business. Add more hours if you need to write partnership agreements, apply for patents, run trademark checks, or do other time-intensive tasks.

Rent deposits are often twice the monthly rent cost. If you plan to rent a property before your business opens its doors, add the cost for these months of rental to the deposit here (e.g., =3000+1500*3 for a deposit and 3 months' rent). Perform a quick search of real-estate listings in your area, and note the source of your information as well as cost.

Supplies costs and working capital can be guesstimated using a round number (e.g., $200 per employee).

License fees, if required in your industry, can usually be identified with a quick web search. Most licenses are annual, but you may want to check for renewal costs and duration now. This information will also be needed in the operating expenses spreadsheet discussed in *Section 6.4: Operating Expenses*.

Sources of Funding

Every dollar you plan to spend before you start selling your product or service must come from a source other than your customers. Expenses can be paid by you (owner's equity), by outside investors, or through loans and credit card debt. Increase the numbers in these columns until your total sources of funding match the total required funds.

People are key to your business and its success. People are often the highest business expense, so it is important to calculate payroll early.

Section 6.2 Payroll

Payroll is often a sizable portion of a business's expenses, so it is calculated early and recalculated often. Sheet 2a invites you to enter the number of employees, average hourly pay, and estimated hours per week for employees in four classifications. Unless you want to calculate further benefits, these are the only cells you need to complete on Sheet 2a or 2b.

All employees must be paid a minimum wage, and non-owner employees should not be expected to work more than 40 hours per week. There is a federal minimum wage, but it is usually lower than state-established minimum wages, many of which are approaching or exceed $15/hr. You can look up your state's minimum-wage timeline, or you can use $15 as your minimum average hourly pay.

Owners can be paid as employees, or they can rely exclusively on profit from the business. Relying on profit is difficult to do in the first few years of your business, however, as few start-ups will be profitable in their first 3–5 years of operation. It is recommended that you pay yourself wages as you first set up your business and that your wages at least match those of any other full-time staff.

Full-time staff and part-time wages are calculated the same because there is no distinction between full-time and part-time at a federal level. Rules may differ at the state level, but generally, full-time employees expect to receive benefits such as health insurance and a retirement plan, whereas part-time employees may not receive benefits.

If you want to pay insurance and other benefits, enter a value from 33% (for hourly rates near $15/hr) to 20% (for hourly rates nearing $40/hr) in the percentage of salary column for employee health insurance.

Independent contractors cost the employer less because some payroll taxes (Social Security and Medicare) are paid by the employee rather than the employer. Independent contractors must have control over their schedule, workload, and workplace, however. They must also work in an industry outside your business's normal pursuits. Consider using independent contractors to accomplish occasional tasks such as creative work and logistics or transportation assistance if these are not part of your business's usual work. See *The Gig Economy* in *Section 3.3* of this text for more on classifying independent contractors.

How much do you need to produce? And how much variety should you start with? Sales forecasts must be made synchronously with payroll decisions if your business is going to be profitable.

Section 6.3 Sales Forecasts

Virtually all business revenue comes from sales, though those sales may come from selling either goods or services. Think back to *Section 2.1: Choosing Business Models*. Can you think of any that are not examples of selling goods or services?

If you have goods or services, they can be considered a product line. If you are a food manufacturer, your product lines might be flavors. If you are a computer refurbisher, your product lines might include basic, premium, or gaming packages. If you repair cars, your product lines might be general categories such as oil changes, brake repair, tires, heating and cooling, transmission work, or other hourly services.

The SCORE Financial Projections Spreadsheet gives room for six product lines. If you have more products in mind, consider how those products can be grouped together by revenue and expenses.

In any service model, be sure to include the costs of parts and labor in your calculations. In the case of a car's oil change, you may decide to only offer synthetic oil changes, calculating the cost of goods sold (COGS) by adding wholesale oil cost ($2 per quart, with an average of six quarts per oil change) to wholesale filter cost ($2) and labor costs (30 minutes at $40/hr). If the COGS for an oil change costs $34 (=2*6+2+40/2), you can safely double this to come up with your sales price per unit. You can further increase sales price, but only to a point. How much do you think you can charge without hurting sales volume? In the case of an oil change, $68 is a fair price for a full-synthetic oil change. If you increase the price further, however, you may price yourself out of the market.

For each product line, calculate COGS and sales price per unit. Then, figure out how many units you would like to sell over the course of your first year. If you were running an auto repair shop, one person could easily do seven oil changes a day, or about 200 oil changes a month. It may prove difficult to get that many customers when you first open, however, so you should be more conservative in calculating the year's average.

Distribute this yearly total across the year in Row 18. If the year's total oil changes is projected to be 1,800 (=150*12), you might hope for 100 oil changes in the first month and plan an additional 10 oil changes each month thereafter. By the time you reach 200 oil changes in the 11th month you would need to lower your prediction for the final month, or you could adapt in another way so the annual total does not exceed the number of units for the year.

Product Lines	Month 1	Month 2	Month 3	Month 4	Month 5	Month 6	Month 7	Month 8	Month 9	Month 10	Month 11	Month 12	Annual Totals
Synthetic													
Oil Changes Sold	100	110	120	130	140	150	160	170	180	190	200	150	1,800
Total Sales	6,800	7,480	8,160	8,840	9,520	10,200	10,880	11,560	12,240	12,920	13,600	10,200	$ 122,400
Total COGS	3,400	3,740	4,080	4,420	4,760	5,100	5,440	5,780	6,120	6,460	6,800	5,100	$ 61,200
Total Margin	3,400	3,740	4,080	4,420	4,760	5,100	5,440	5,780	6,120	6,460	6,800	5,100	$ 61,200

Table 6.3.1. 1,800 oil changes distributed across a year of sales. Although no forecast is likely to prove true, it will hopefully be close. For the forecast here to come true, an auto shop owner would want to invest heavily in advertising for the first few months of business.

When you have finished distributing all your product lines' sales across Year 1, you can turn your attention to Years 2 and 3. The spreadsheet that includes Years 2 and 3 takes the value from the same month in Year 1 and increases it by the growth rate defined at the top of the page. If you are only concerned about numbers being accurate at the end of the year, this is a fine method. You can choose a growth rate that is representative of your business (e.g., 20% for the first few years of an average start-up) and let the spreadsheet do its work.

If it is important for you to know in which month your business will become profitable (as we will discuss in *Section 6.5: Financial Analyses*), you may want to start with where you left off in Year 1 and calculate your own growth rates by product line. If you continue thinking about oil changes, it might be reasonable for an employee to do 15 oil changes a day. If you think the market will provide enough vehicles, you could have the pace of oil changes continue to increase by 10 additional oil changes a month through at least Year 2.

Before you consider your work on sales forecasts to be completed, however, you should revisit your payroll. If you expect the number of oil changes to increase beyond what one employee can handle, have you also increased the number of employees? Carefully consider how the sales forecast for each of your product lines might impact staffing needs, and make changes accordingly.

Legal fees are often an overlooked operating expense. New business owners should not forget to account for legal expenses, advertising, insurance, licenses, maintenance, and regular financial reviews by a CPA.

Section 6.4 Operating Expenses

The expenses we included as part of our sales forecast were variable expenses: expenses that change alongside production or sales volume. Although the cost of goods sold is an important one, there are many other fixed costs that are required to "keep the lights on."

Advertising is often one of the largest operating expenses for a new business because you will need to spend money for customers to recognize your name or brand. Advertising should be measured in the hundreds or thousands of dollars. If you are a start-up, it should start high, and you should maintain spending at high levels throughout the first year of your business.

You began thinking about many of the other expense categories earlier. Car/truck expenses, legal/professional services, licenses, office/equipment expenses, supplies, and utilities were all addressed in *Section 6.1: Start-Up Expenses*. Remember that licenses and legal/professional services will often be annual expenses. Legal services will be highest at start-up, but you should set money aside to address legal questions or lawsuits as you conduct business.

Business insurance is another important consideration. Business insurance is there to protect you in unexpected situations such as flooding, fire, or theft. Liability insurance protects you if someone gets injured at work or on your property. Some states require insurance for businesses in different industries, but it is a good idea to have some level of coverage.

The only way to get a good idea of insurance costs is to talk to an insurance agent (or several!). For a poor estimate, you can consider the level of risk at your business—start at $60/mo for a risk-free office, adding $10/mo per additional employee. Start at $120/mo if your business uses any form of heavy equipment, adding $20/mo per employee.

If your business will have contractors working directly with customers, or if non-employees will be on site, increase costs by another $40–120/mo depending on the risk inherent in your industry.

Be sure you have included some round-number estimates for supplies and miscellaneous expenses. Every business will also have costs for repairs and maintenance, even if those dollars are only needed to paint the walls every few years. Raise your guesstimate for repairs and maintenance to reflect the number of on-site employees and the role that vehicles and equipment play in your business.

When you have completed Sheet 5a, also complete Sheet 5b. Here, you just need to update the growth rate. Three percent is a little above the average amount of inflation in the U.S. dollar from year to year, but prices for goods often rise outside of inflation. A 3% estimate may fall on the low end, or a 5% growth rate will generally cover all likely cost increases.

Before you leave your operating expenses, take a look back at the values under operating capital in Sheet 1. Do your start-up expense estimates still make sense?

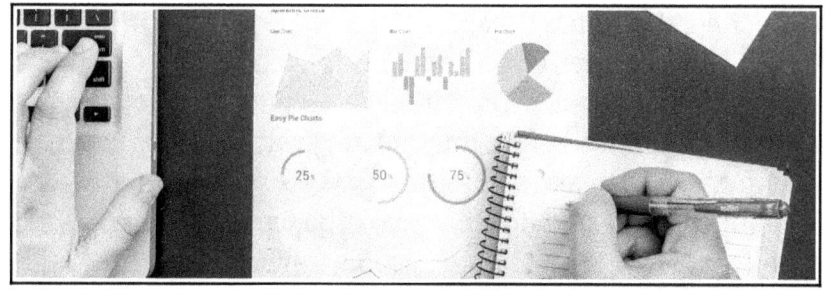

There are many ways to bring together the values from earlier sections, but graphs only represent one of them.

Section 6.5 Financial Analyses

If you have made it this far, you have likely completed all the sections of your financial projections. Congratulations!

Unfortunately, your work may not be finished. We looked at revenue and expenses separately, and to fully understand the state of your business, we need to look at them together.

To begin your financial analysis, look at the net income/loss at the bottom of your income statement on Sheet 7b. In SCORE's spreadsheet, negative numbers are set to display in parentheses (e.g., **(1,000)**). One way to measure the health of your proposed business is to ensure your business has a net income by Year 3. A net income does not mean your business will be profitable overall, but it means your business will likely be profitable in its first 5 years, even if you cannot see profitability in the first 3 years.

To consider profitability, look at your cash flow statements (Sheet 6b and/or Sheet 6a). Your business has reached profitability when your ending cash balance has exceeded the line of credit balance. It is possible that this point does not occur in the first 3 years, or it is possible that it is achieved and then it falters. If your cash balance begins to decline, that is a red flag.

Other measures of business health can be found in the financial ratios sheet. You will have seen the first few profitability ratios before, but the net profit margin, return on equity (ROE), and return on assets (ROA) are all new, valuable readings on how well your business is doing. Ideally, none of these numbers should ever be negative, and your net profit margin should be above 10% every year. A 10% net profit margin would mean that for every dollar in sales, 10 cents is profit after all expenses.

In addition to the red flags provided by a declining cash balance, a negative or declining ROE, a negative or declining ROA, or a low net profit margin, days in inventory can provide insight into your business's efficiency. A perfect days in inventory measure would be 0 (the product has a buyer as soon as it is produced), but it may be ideal to have a few days of inventory on hand at all times to accommodate unexpected problems.

If your business does not have a net income by the end of Year 3, or if you have identified any other red flags, you will want to revisit the numbers from the other sheets. To increase your business's profitability, can you increase your gross margin (by decreasing COGS or increasing sales price)? Can you decrease payroll (by changing pay rates or hours worked per week)? Can you lower other operating expenses? Remember that changes in payroll can affect the possible output of your sales projections, as can changes in some of your expenses, especially advertising.

If you need help identifying, understanding, or fixing any problems in your financial analyses, reach out to experts near you, including instructors or advisors for the U.S. Small Business Administration (SBA).

References

1.0 Introduction
Daly, L. (2024, August 4). *The largest companies by market cap in 2024*. The Motley Fool. https://www.fool.com/research/largest-companies-by-market-cap/

1.1 A Common Vocabulary
Harvard Business School Institute for Strategy & Competitiveness. (2023). *The value chain*. https://www.isc.hbs.edu/strategy/business-strategy/Pages/the-value-chain.aspx

Laudon, K., & Traver, C. (2022). The revolution is just beginning. In *E-Commerce 2021: Business, technology, and society* (15th ed.). Pearson.

1.2 A Brief History of E-Commerce
Freiberger, P. A., & Swaine, M. R. (2023, August 1). *Computer: History of computing*. Britannica. https://www.britannica.com/technology/computer/History-of-computing

Furlan, J., & Garcia, C. (2020, November 11). *The lessons of Pets.com* [Radio broadcast]. NPR. https://www.npr.org/2020/11/11/933951757/the-lessons-of-pets-com

IBM. (2023). *What is electronic data interchange?* https://www.ibm.com/topics/edi-electronic-data-interchange

Schneider, G. (2017). Introduction to electronic commerce. In *Electronic commerce* (12th ed.). Cengage Learning.

UN/EDIFACT. (2023, June 30). In *Gale Encyclopedia of E-Commerce*. https://www.encyclopedia.com/economics/encyclopedias-almanacs-transcripts-and-maps/unedifact

Zhang, M. (2008, February 6). *ActionScript libraries help mashing up the web 2.0 platforms*. InfoQ. https://www.infoq.com/news/2008/02/actionscript-libs-for-mashup/

1.3 A Legal History of E-Commerce

Adler, A. (2023, May 26). *The Supreme Court's Warhol decision just changed the future of art.* Art News. https://www.artnews.com/art-in-america/columns/supreme-court-andy-warhol-decision-appropriation-artists-impact-1234669718

Bensinger, G., & Scarcella, M. (2023, December 13). *Epic Games wins antitrust case against Google over Play app store.* Reuters. https://www.reuters.com/legal/google-epic-games-face-off-app-antitrust-trial-nears-end-2023-12-11/

Brodkin, J. (2023, April 25). *EU names 19 large tech platforms that must follow Europe's new Internet rules.* Ars Technica. https://arstechnica.com/tech-policy/2023/04/google-runs-5-of-the-19-platforms-that-must-follow-eus-new-internet-rules/

Calingaert, D. (2010, April 1). *Authoritarianism vs. the Internet: The race between freedom and repression.* Hoover Institution, Stanford University. https://www.hoover.org/research/authoritarianism-vs-internet

Chow, S. Y. (2017). A snapshot of online contracting two decades after ProCD v. Zeidenberg. *The Business Lawyer, 73*(1), 267–276. https://www.jstor.org/stable/10.2307/26419205

Downes, L. (2017, March 31). *The tangled web of net neutrality and regulation.* Harvard Business Review. https://hbr.org/2017/03/the-tangled-web-of-net-neutrality-and-regulation

European Commission. (2023, July 7). *Q&A: DMA: Ensuring fair and open digital markets.* https://ec.europa.eu/commission/presscorner/detail/en/qanda_20_2349

Exec. Order No. 13904, 85 Fed. Reg. 6725 (2020, January 31). https://www.federalregister.gov/d/2020-02439

Exec. Order No. 14036, 86 Fed. Reg. 36987 (2021, July 9). https://www.federalregister.gov/d/2021-15069

Exec. Order No. 14067, 87 Fed. Reg. 14143 (2022, March 9). https://www.federalregister.gov/d/2022-05471

Flynn, K. (2021, February 19). *Facebook bans news in Australia as fight with government escalates.* CNN. https://edition.cnn.com/2021/02/17/media/facebook-australia-news-ban/

Gonzalez v. Google LLC, 598 U.S. ____ (2023). https://www.supremecourt.gov/opinions/22pdf/21-1333_6j7a.pdf

Liedtke, M. (2024, January 16). *Supreme Court rebuffs Apple's appeal on app payments, threatening billions in revenue.* Associated Press. https://apnews.com/article/supreme-court-apple-epic-fortnite-antitrust-iphone-c412553d88f8798acd7d5e1cbb5826bc

Lovendale, R., & Lam, K. V. (2022, August 10). *Recent court decisions shed light on enforceability of electronic contracts in the U.S.* Goodwin Procter LLP. https://www.goodwinlaw.com/en/insights/publications/2022/08/08_10-recent-court-decisions-shed-light

Newton, C. (2020, December 29). *Everything you need to know about Section 230.* The Verge. https://www.theverge.com/21273768/section-230-explained-internet-speech-law-definition-guide-free-moderation

The World Factbook. (2023, July 6). *Countries.* Central Intelligence Agency. https://www.cia.gov/the-world-factbook/countries/

Twitter, Inc. v. Taamneh, 598 U.S. ____ (2023). https://www.supremecourt.gov/opinions/22pdf/21-1496_d18f.pdf

1.4 The State of E-Commerce Today

Activision Blizzard. (2023, February 6). *Activision Blizzard announces fourth quarter and 2022 financial results.* https://investor.activision.com/news-releases/news-release-details/activision-blizzard-announces-fourth-quarter-and-2022-financial

Anderson, C. (2006). The long tail. In *The long tail: Why the future of business is selling less of more.* Hyperion.

Brock, D. C., & Grad, B. (2022). Expert systems: Commercializing artificial intelligence. *IEEE Annals of the History of Computing, 44*(1), 5–7. http://dx.doi.org/10.1109/MAHC.2022.3149612

IBM Data and AI Team. (2023, October 12). *Understanding the different types of artificial intelligence.* IBM. https://ibm.com/think/topics/artificial-intelligence-types

Laudon, K., & Traver, C. (2022). Ethical, social, and political issues in e-commerce. In *E-Commerce 2021: Business, technology, and society* (15th ed.). Pearson.

Metacritic. (2023a). *Diablo Immortal for PC.* Retrieved August 6, 2023 from https://www.metacritic.com/game/pc/diablo-immortal/user-reviews

Metacritic. (2023b). *Diablo III: Reaper of souls for PC.* Retrieved August 6, 2023 from https://metacritic.com/game/diablo-iii-reaper-of-souls/

Pitchbook. (2023, January 20). *Bread Beauty Supply company profile.* https://pitchbook.com/profiles/company/287844-40

UN Economic Commission for Africa. (2021, March). *COVID-19 Impact on e-commerce: Africa.* https://hdl.handle.net/10855/43939

Yang, Z. (2022, November 22). *China just announced a new social credit law. Here's what it means.* MIT Technology Review. https://www.technologyreview.com/2022/11/22/1063605/china-announced-a-new-social-credit-law-what-does-it-mean/

CS1 Building & Bending e-Commerce

Buskirk, E. V. (2009, September 22). *How the Netflix Prize was won.* Wired. https://www.wired.com/2009/09/how-the-netflix-prize-was-won/

Katwala, A. (2020, September 16). *Why are 2 million people still getting Netflix DVDs by mail?* Wired. https://wired.com/story/why-are-2-million-people-still-getting-netflix-dvds-by-mail/

McFadden, C. (2023, March 1). *From DVDs to streaming, here's the incredible story of Netflix.* Interesting Engineering. https://interestingengineering.com/culture/the-fascinating-history-of-netflix

Randolph, M. (2019). *That will never work: The birth of Netflix and the amazing life of an idea*. Octopus. [see pp. 141, 215–217, 268–269]

Roettgers, J. (2023, September 25). *The high tech behind Netflix's old-school DVD service*. The Verge. https://theverge.com/23883662/netflix-dvd-shutdown-complex-tech-packaging-mail

Sandvine. *The Global Internet Phenomena Report*. (2023, January). https://sandvine.com/hubfs/Sandvine_Redesign_2019/Downloads/2023/reports/Sandvine%20GIPR%202023.pdf

Shmatikov, V., & Narayanan, A. (2008, February 5). *How to break anonymity of the Netflix Prize dataset* (2nd ed.). ArXiv. https://doi.org/10.48550/arXiv.cs/0610105

Singel, R. (2009). *Netflix spilled your Brokeback Mountain secret, lawsuit claims*. Wired. https://www.wired.com/2009/12/netflix-privacy-lawsuit/

Video Privacy Protection Act of 1988, 18 U.S.C. § 2710. (1988).

Video Privacy Protection Act Amendment, 18 U.S.C. § 2710. (2013).

2.0 Initial Business Tasks

Tarver, E. (2023, April 18). *Horizontal integration vs. vertical integration: Key differences*. Investopedia. https://www.investopedia.com/ask/answers/051315/what-difference-between-horizontal-integration-and-vertical-integration.asp

2.1 An Overview of Business Models

Laudon, K., & Traver, C. (2022). E-Commerce business models and concepts. In *E-Commerce 2021: Business, technology, and society* (15th ed.). Pearson.

U.S. Small Business Administration. (2023, May 19). *Choose a business structure*. https://www.sba.gov/business-guide/launch-your-business/choose-business-structure

U.S. Small Business Administration. (2023, June 12). *Write your business plan.* https://www.sba.gov/business-guide/plan-your-business/write-your-business-plan

2.2 Choosing a Revenue Model
Amazon Associates. (2022). *Amazon.com Associates central.* https://affiliate-program.amazon.com/

Hood & Strong, LLP. (2023, September 6). *Mozilla Foundation and subsidiaries: Independent auditor's report and consolidated financial statements.* https://assets.mozilla.net/annualreport/2022/mozilla-fdn-2022-fs-final-0908.pdf

Rappa, M. (2023, April 18). *Business models on the web.* Digital Enterprise. https://digitalenterprise.org/models/

2.3 Identifying Target Markets
Library of Congress. (2023, August 15). *Doing consumer research: Market segments.* https://guides.loc.gov/consumer-research/market-segments

Yamane, T., & Kaneko, S. (2021, April). Is the younger generation a driving force toward achieving the sustainable development goals? Survey experiments. *Journal of Cleaner Production, 292.* https://doi.org/10.1016/j.jclepro.2021.125932

2.4 Crafting a Corporate Message
Cox, L. K. (2023, May 11). *32 mission and vision statement examples that will inspire your buyers.* https://blog.hubspot.com/marketing/inspiring-company-mission-statements

IKEA. (2023). *About us.* Retrieved August 20, 2023 from https://about.ikea.com/en/about-us

Southwest Airlines. (2023). *About us.* Retrieved August 20, 2023 from https://www.southwest.com/about-southwest/

Tesla. (2023). *About us.* Retrieved August 20, 2023 from https://www.tesla.com/about

2.5 Conducting Market Research

Armitage, J., & Roberts, J. (2019). The globalisation of luxury fashion: The case of Gucci. *Luxury, 6*(3), 227–246. https://doi.org/10.1080/20511817.2021.1897268

Bose. (2023, August 19). *QuietComfort 45 noise cancelling headphones.* https://www.bose.com/p/headphones/bose-quietcomfort-45-headphones/QC45-HEADPHONEARN-BLK-WW.html

Katz, L. (2022, March 1). *Sennheiser HD 450BT review.* SoundGuys. https://www.soundguys.com/sennheiser-hd-450bt-review-39828/

Katz, L. (2022, March 18). *House of Marley Exodus review.* SoundGuys. https://www.soundguys.com/house-of-marley-exodus-review-22910/

Lamb, C. W., Hair, J. F., & McDaniel, C. (2021). Advertising, public relations, and sales promotion. In *MKTG* (13th ed.). Cengage.

Levin, T. (2022, November 21). *Car companies want to make billions by charging monthly fees for features like heated seats, but buyers won't pay up.* Business Insider. https://www.businessinsider.com/car-feature-subscriptions-add-ons-bmw-ford-toyota-gm-2022-2

Ralston, J. (n.d.). *House of Marley Exodus ANC: Wireless Bluetooth over-ear headphones with active noise-canceling.* Crutchfield. Retrieved August 21, 2023 from https://www.crutchfield.com/S-b4StIqsKR4B/p_346EXDUSNC/House-of-Marley-Exodus-ANC.html

Sennheiser. (n.d.). *HD 450BT.* Retrieved August 21, 2023 from https://www.sennheiser-hearing.com/en-US/p/hd-450bt/

Sony. (n.d.). *Sony WH-1000XM5 wireless noise cancelling headphones.* Retrieved August 21, 2023 from https://electronics.sony.com/audio/headphones/headband/p/wh1000xm5-b

Symphonized. (n.d.). *Wraith 2.0 wireless: Walnut.* Retrieved August 21, 2023 from https://symphonized.com/products/wraith-2-0-wireless

Thomas, C. (2023, June 30). *Bose QuietComfort 45 review: Great ANC, odd sound*. SoundGuys. https://www.soundguys.com/bose-quietcomfort-45-review-60657/

Thomas, C. (2023, July 28). *Sony WH-1000XMS review*. SoundGuys. https://www.soundguys.com/sony-wh-1000xm5-review-71783/

CS2 Products Plus Programs

Fowler, S. (2023, April 27). Precision agriculture technology helps farmers - but they need help. National Public Radio. https://www.npr.org/2023/04/27/1172434673/precision-agriculture-technology-helps-farmers-but-they-need-help

Goedde, L., Katz, J., Ménard, A., & Revellat, J. (2020, October 9). *Agriculture's connected future: How technology can yield new growth*. McKinsey & Company. https://mckinsey.com/industries/agriculture/our-insights/agricultures-connected-future-how-technology-can-yield-new-growth

John Deere US. (n.d.) *About our company*. Retrieved July 28, 2024 from https://www.deere.com/en/website/our-company/

John Deere US. (2022, November 15). *John Deere data services & subscriptions statement*. https://www.deere.com/en/privacy-and-data/data-services/index.html

John Deere US. (2024, July 7). *John Deere*. Facebook. Retrieved July 7, 2024 from https://facebook.com/JohnDeereUSCA

Mississippi River/Gulf of Mexico Watershed Nutrient Task Force. (2008). *Gulf hypoxia action plan 2008 for reducing, mitigating, and controlling hypoxia in the northern Gulf of Mexico and improving water quality in the Mississippi River Basin*. https://epa.gov/sites/default/files/2015-03/documents/2008_8_28_msbasin_ghap2008_update082608.pdf

Mulla, D., & Khosla, R. (2016). Historical evolution and recent advances in precision farming. In *Soil-specific farming: Precision agriculture*. Routledge.

NovAtel. *High-precision GNSS for precision agriculture banner* [image]. https://novatel.com/-/media/Images/Hexagon/Hexagon%20Core/Novatel/assestsFinal/assets/Web-Phase-2-2012/Industry-Pages/Agriculture/AG-Banner-1680x885.ashx

Paarlberg, R. (2023). Sustainable food and farming: When public perceptions depart from science. In D. Resnick, & J. F. M. Swinnen (Eds.), *The political economy of food transformation: Pathways to progress in a polarized world* (pp. 230–251). Oxford University Press.

U.S. Government Accountability Office. (2024, January 31). Precision agriculture: Benefits and challenges for technology adoption and use. https://www.gao.gov/products/gao-24-105962

3.0 Finding Stakeholders

Harris Insights & Analytics LLC. (2021, May). 2021 Norton cyber safety insights report global results. https://us.norton.com/content/dam/norton/pdfs/reports/2021_nortonLifelock_cyber_safety_insights_report_global_results.pdf

Kelly, M., & Williams, C. (2015). The marketing environment. In *BUSN⁷: Introduction to business* (7th ed., pp. 179–180).

3.1 Talking to Investors

Laudon, K., & Traver, C. (2022). E-Commerce business models and concepts. In *E-Commerce 2021: Business, technology, and society* (15th ed.). Pearson.

MacDonald, S. (2023, April 4). *How to write a winning sales pitch (in less than 10 minutes)*. SuperOffice. https://www.superoffice.com/blog/sales-pitch/

SCORE Association. (2013, January 13). SCORE financial projections guide. http://s3.amazonaws.com/mentoring.redesign/s3fs-public/Financial%2520Projections%2520Template%2520Guide%2520-%2520English.pdf

SCORE Association. (2023, May). *Financial projections template* [Microsoft Excel spreadsheet]. https://score.org/sites/default/files/2023-05/SCORE%20Financial%20Projections

U.S. Small Business Administration. (2023, June 2). *Choose your business name*. https://www.sba.gov/business-guide/launch-your-business/choose-your-business-name

U.S. Small Business Administration. (2024, April 8). *Write your business plan.* https://www.sba.gov/business-guide/plan-your-business/write-your-business-plan

3.2 Pre- and Post-Investor Analyses

Albee, J. (2019, June 20). A.B.C.D. of learning objectives. Hannibal-LaGrange University. https://www.hlg.edu/wp-content/uploads/2019/06/ABCD-of-Learning-Objectives-Summer-2019.pdf

Kelly, M., & Williams, C. (2015). The marketing environment. In *BUSN⁷: Introduction to business* (7th ed., p. 179–180).

Leonard, K., & Watts, R. (2024, May 30). *The ultimate guide to S.M.A.R.T. goals.* Forbes. https://www.forbes.com/advisor/business/smart-goals/

Schneider, G. (2017). Identifying electronic commerce opportunities. In *Electronic commerce* (12th ed.). Cengage Learning.

3.3 Hiring Talent

Faculty of Arts and Sciences Human Resources Department. (2015, April 2). *Guide to legally permissible interview questions and discussions.* https://hr.fas.harvard.edu/files/fas-hr/files/appendix_e_guide_to_legally_permissible_interview_questions_and_discussions_03202015.pdf

U.S. Department of Labor. (2024, March 11). Fact sheet 13: employee or independent contractor classification under the Fair Labor Standards Act (FLSA). https://www.dol.gov/agencies/whd/fact-sheets/13-flsa-employment-relationship

3.4 Stakeholder Privacy

Beasley, J. S., & Nilkaew, P. (2022). Network Security. In *Networking essentials: A CompTIA(TM) Network+ N10-008 textbook* (6th ed., p. 606–610). Pearson.

Fruhlinger, J. (2024, May 17). DDoS attacks: Definition, examples, and techniques. CSO. https://www.csoonline.com/article/571981/ddos-attacks-definition-examples-and-techniques.html

Lanfear, T., McClister, C., Piesco, J., Tran, J., Berry, D., Lehr, B., Wassenaar, B., Baldwin, M., & Kess, B. (2023, February 13). *Azure facilities, premises, and physical security.* Microsoft Learn. https://learn.microsoft.com/en-us/azure/security/fundamentals/physical-security

Mitnick, K. D. (2002). *The art of deception: Controlling the human element of security.* Pearson.

CS3 Concerning Sharks

Buxton, R. (2023, March 3). *What's it really like to be a contestant on "Shark Tank"?* Katie Couric Media. https://katiecouric.com/entertainment/movies-tv/whats-it-like-to-be-on-shark-tank-behind-the-scenes/

Episode #14.10 (Season 14, Episode 10) [TV series episode]. (2023, January 6). In L. Freiner, Y. Lingner, D. Lorenz, M. Morlath, & M. Swedlow (Executive Producers), *Shark Tank.* Mark Burnett Productions; Sony Pictures Television.

Keveney, B. (2019, September 29). *'Shark Tank' secrets: Life-changing moments on an assembly line of product pitches.* USA Today. https://www.usatoday.com/story/entertainment/tv/2019/09/27/shark-tank-deals-get-bigger-bolder-going-into-season-11/2445384001/

Nippon TV. (2021, February 22). *Nippon TV format "Dragons' Den" to air on BBC One.* https://www.ntv.co.jp/english/pressrelease/20210222.html

Spears, D. (2024, January 24). *JicaFoods Shark Tank update: How they're changing snacking forever.* Silicon Spice. https://siliconspice.com/jicafoods-shark-tank-update/

4.0 Building a Web Site

Schneider, G. (2017). Electronic commerce: Opportunities, cautions, and concerns. In *Electronic commerce* (12th ed.). Cengage Learning.

4.1 Web Infrastructure

Adee, S. (2019, May 14). BBC News. *The global Internet is disintegrating: what comes next?*. https://www.bbc.com/future/article/20190514-the-global-internet-is-disintegrating-what-comes-next

Bali, K. (2020, April 21). *What is IPv6? Why you should start using it now?* ServerGuy. https://serverguy.com/servers/what-is-ipv6/

Beasley, J. S., & Nilkaew, P. (2022). Managing the Network Infrastructure. In *Networking essentials: A CompTIA(TM) Network+ N10-008 textbook* (6th ed., p. 606–610). Pearson.

Downes, L. (2018, April 9). *GDPR and the end of the Internet's grand bargain*. Harvard Business Review. https://hbr.org/2018/04/gdpr-and-the-end-of-the-internets-grand-bargain

Google. (2024, August 7). *IPv6 statistics*. https://google.com/intl/en/ipv6/statistics.html

Jackson, J. (2023, February 2). *EU analyst: The end of the Internet is near*. The New Stack. https://thenewstack.io/eu-analyst-the-end-of-the-internet-is-near/

Jefferson Online. (2016, November 22). *From ARPANET to World Wide Web: An Internet history timeline*. Thomas Jefferson University. https://online.jefferson.edu/business/internet-history-timeline/

4.2 Web Hosts

Beasley, J. S., & Nilkaew, P. (2022). Managing the network infrastructure. In *Networking essentials: A CompTIA(TM) Network+ N10-008 textbook* (6th ed., p. 606–610). Pearson.

Cloudflare. (2022). *Five best practices for mitigating DDoS attacks*. https://cf-assets.www.cloudflare.com/slt3lc6tev37/58Znmio29pRXDLKoQgNIz4/5cf1a6d3b1b1f5f1ea995460e04eb512/BDES-2587-Design-Wrap-Refreshed-DDoS-White-Paper-Letter.pdf

IONOS. (2023, March 22). *SSD vs. HDD*. https://ionos.com/digitalguide/server/know-how/ssd-vs-hdd/

4.3 Web Navigation

Design guidelines for the web. (2006). UsabilityNet. http://usabilitynet.org/tools/webdesign.htm

Hagaman, M., & McHenry, K. (2015). *Graphic design for 21st century presentations: Integrated art & technology curriculum.* On-Demand Publishing, LLC.

U.S. Web Design System. (2024, June 27). *Design principles.* https://designsystem.digital.gov/design-principles/

4.4 Web Design

Glassman, E., Guo, P., Jackson, D., Karger, D., Kim, J., Miller, R., Mueller, S., Sims, C., & Zhang, H. (2021, October 15). Reading 8: Prototyping. MIT. http://web.mit.edu/6.813/www/sp17/classes/08-prototyping/

Hagaman, M., & McHenry, K. (2015). *Graphic design for 21st century presentations: Integrated art & technology curriculum.* On-Demand Publishing, LLC.

Minnick, J. (2021). Introduction to the Internet and web design. In *Responsive web design with HTML 5 and CSS* (9th ed., p 1–45). Cengage.

Randolph, M. (2019). *That will never work: The birth of Netflix and the amazing life of an idea.* Octopus. [see pp. 141]

U.S. Web Design System. (2024, June 27). *Design principles.* https://designsystem.digital.gov/design-principles/

4.5 Web Development

Accessibility. (2024, June 21). Mozilla Developer Network. https://developer.mozilla.org/en-US/docs/Web/Accessibility

Ecograder. (2024, July 27). *Impact report for https://web.dev/articles/choose-js-library-or-framework.* https://ecograder.com/report/DBV3AdEuGtYRvJ9N5HD3qn9u

O'Hara, S., Lauke, P. H., & Faulkner, S. (Eds.) (2024, May 7). *ARIA in HTML.* World Wide Web Consortium. https://www.w3.org/TR/html-aria/

U.S. Department of Justice Civil Rights Division. (2022, March 18). *Guidance on Web Accessibility and the ADA.* ADA.gov. https://www.ada.gov/resources/web-guidance/

W3Techs. (2024a, August 7). *Usage statistics and market shares of content management systems*. https://w3techs.com/technologies/overview/content_management

W3Techs. (2024b, August 7). *Usage statistics and market shares of operating systems for websites*. https://w3techs.com/technologies/overview/operating_system

W3Techs. (2024c, August 7). *Usage statistics and market shares of web servers*. https://w3techs.com/technologies/overview/web_server

W3Techs. (2024d, August 7). *Usage statistics of server-side programming languages for websites*. https://w3techs.com/technologies/overview/programming_language

World Wide Web Consortium. (2023, October 5). *Web Content Accessibility Guidelines (WCAG) 2.2*. https://www.w3.org/TR/WCAG22/

4.6 Web Analytics

Awichanirost, J., & Phumchusri, N. (2020). Analyzing the effects of sessions on unique visitors and unique page views with Google Analytics: A case study of a tourism website in Thailand. *2020 IEEE 7th International Conference on Industrial Engineering and Applications (*pp. 1014–1018). https://doi.org/10.1109/ICIEA49774.2020.9102094

Merriam, S. B., & Tisdell, E. J. (2016). What is qualitative research? In *Qualitative research: A guide to design and implementation* (4th ed., pp. 3–21). Jossey-Bass.

Mortati, M., Magistretti, S., Cautela, C., & Dell'Era, C. (2023, April). Data in design: How big data and thick data inform design thinking projects. *Technovation, 122*. https://doi.org/10.1016/j.technovation.2022.102688

CS4 Industrial Analytics

Foote, K. D. (2022, January 14). *A brief history of the Internet of Things*. Dataversity. https://www.dataversity.net/brief-history-internet-things/

Garbrecht, S. (2017, October 30). *Better together: APM and MES applied in manufacturing.* GE Digital Solutions. https://ge.com/digital/sites/default/files/download_assets/Better%20together.pdf

GE Digital Solutions. (2018, August 14). *Predix MES production manager screenshot* [image]. https://www.ge.com/digital/sites/default/files/screenshot-Predix-MES-Production-Manager-1792x1280.jpg

GE Digital Solutions. (2023a, March 31). *Accessing cloud message queue web console.* https://www.ge.com/digital/documentation/predix-platforms/cmq-web-console.html

GE Digital Solutions. (2023b, March 31). *What is Predix platform?* https://www.ge.com/digital/documentation/predix-platforms/c_what_is_predix_platform.html

GE Digital Solutions. (2024, July 16). *Edge OS architecture.* https://www.ge.com/digital/documentation/edge-software/c_predix_edge_os_architecture.html

Mortati, M., Magistretti, S., Cautela, C., & Dell'Era, C. (2023, April). Data in design: How big data and thick data inform design thinking projects. *Technovation, 122.* https://doi.org/10.1016/j.technovation.2022.102688

Wining, L. (2016, February 18). *GE's big bet on data and analytics: Seeking opportunities in the Internet of Things, GE expands into industrial analytics.* MIT Sloan Management Review. https://sloanreview.mit.edu/case-study/ge-big-bet-on-data-and-analytics/

5.0 Communicating with Stakeholders

American Marketing Association. (2022, July 12). *The four Ps of marketing.* https://www.ama.org/marketing-news/the-four-ps-of-marketing/

5.1 Marketing Strategies

Amazon. (2024, February 12). *How to sell on Amazon: A guide for beginners.* https://sell.amazon.com/beginners-guide.html

Amazon. (2024, January 30). *Amazon's approach to controversial products and content.* https://www.aboutamazon.com/news/how-amazon-works/amazons-approach-to-controversial-products-and-content

Kopp, C. M. (2024, February 26). *Product life cycle explained: Stages and examples.* Investopedia. https://www.investopedia.com/terms/p/product-life-cycle.asp

Lamb, C. W., Hair, J. F., & McDaniel, C. (2021a). Advertising, public relations, and sales promotion. In *MKTG^{13}: Principles of marketing* (13th ed., pp. 288–309). Cengage.

Lamb, C. W., Hair, J. F., & McDaniel, C. (2021b). Developing and managing products. In *MKTG^{13}: Principles of marketing* (13th ed., pp. 194–209). Cengage.

Lamb, C. W., Hair, J. F., & McDaniel, C. (2021c). Marketing communications. In *MKTG^{13}: Principles of marketing* (13th ed., pp. 270–287). Cengage.

Lamb, C. W., Hair, J. F., & McDaniel, C. (2021d). Product concepts. In *MKTG^{13}: Principles of marketing* (13th ed., pp. 178–193). Cengage.

Lamb, C. W., Hair, J. F., & McDaniel, C. (2021e). Retailing. In *MKTG^{13}: Principles of marketing* (13th ed., pp. 250–269). Cengage.

Lamb, C. W., Hair, J. F., & McDaniel, C. (2021f). Supply chain management and marketing channels. In *MKTG^{13}: Principles of marketing* (13th ed., pp. 224–249). Cengage.

5.2 Advertising Strategies

Curlee, E. (2009, January 23). *LifeLock customer selling v1.* SlideShare. https://www.slideshare.net/slideshow/LifeLockCustomerSellingv1/947921

DeVries, H. (2022, January 17). *7 biggest online advertising blunders.* Forbes. https://forbes.com/sites/henrydevries/2022/01/16/7-biggest-online-advertising-blunders/

Fessenden, T. (2017, June 4). *The most hated online advertising techniques.* Nielsen Norman Group. https://nngroup.com/articles/most-hated-advertising-techniques/

Lamb, C. W., Hair, J. F., & McDaniel, C. (2021a). Advertising, public relations, and sales promotion. In *MKTG¹³: Principles of marketing* (13th ed., pp. 288–309). Cengage.

Lamb, C. W., Hair, J. F., & McDaniel, C. (2021b). Marketing analytics. In *MKTG¹³: Principles of marketing* (13th ed., pp. 370–377). Cengage.

Lamb, C. W., Hair, J. F., & McDaniel, C. (2021c). Marketing communications. In *MKTG¹³: Principles of marketing* (13th ed., pp. 270–287). Cengage.

Marino, S. (2024, August 2). *Facebook ads benchmarks for 2023: New data + insights for your industry.* LocaliQ. https://www.wordstream.com/blog/ws/2023/11/28/facebook-ads-benchmarks

Marino, S. (2024, June 10). *Google Ads benchmarks 2024: New trends & insights for key industries.* LocaliQ. https://www.wordstream.com/blog/2024-google-ads-benchmarks

Morgan, S. (2016, May 2). *LifeLock reboots after agreeing to pay $100 million, settling FTC charges of deceptive advertising.* Forbes. https://www.forbes.com/sites/stevemorgan/2016/05/02/lifelock-reboots-after-agreeing-to-pay-100-million-settling-ftc-charges-of-deceptive-advertising/

Pivotal Health Solutions. (2015, August 14). *8 examples of brilliant health care marketing.* http://pivotalhealthsolutions.com/mobile/learn/blog/8-examples-of-brilliant-health-care-marketing.aspx

Stern, R. (2010, May 13). *Cracking LifeLock: Even after a $12 million penalty for deceptive advertising, the Tempe company can't be honest about its identity-theft-protection service.* Phoenix New Times. https://phoenixnewtimes.com/news/cracking-lifelock-even-after-a-12-million-penalty-for-deceptive-advertising-the-tempe-company-cant-be-honest-about-its-identity-theft-protection-service-6445863

Tesseras, L. (2018, October 26). *How LADbible got people to fight plastic pollution by creating a country.* MarketingWeek. https://marketingweek.com/ladbible-trash-isles-campaign/

U.S. Federal Trade Commission. (2010, March 9). *LifeLock will pay $12 million to settle charges by the FTC and 35 states that identity theft prevention and data security claims were false.* https://www.ftc.gov/news-events/news/press-releases/2010/03/lifelock-will-pay-12-million-settle-charges-ftc-35-states-identity-theft-prevention-data-security

Userpilot. (2024, June 29). *Average customer acquisition cost: Benchmark by industry and how to improve it.* https://userpilot.com/blog/average-customer-acquisition-cost/

5.3 Social Media

Auxier, B., & Anderson, M. (2021, April 7). *Social media use in 2021.* Pew Research Center. https://pewresearch.org/internet/2021/04/07/social-media-use-in-2021/

Fernando, J. (2024, May 16). *Return on Investment (ROI): How to calculate it and what it means.* Investopedia. https://investopedia.com/terms/r/returnoninvestment.asp

Malik, U. (2015, May 4). Pros and cons of social media marketing for business. LinkedIn. https://www.linkedin.com/pulse/pros-cons-social-media-marketing-business-malik-4000-

Pew Research Center. (2021, February 8). *Social media use.* https://www.pewresearch.org/internet/chart/social-media-use/

Rubin, T. (2011, April 5). Return on Relationship: The new measure of success. http://tedrubin.com/return-on-relationship-the-new-measure-of-success/

Buckingham Design Associates. (2010, October 5). What are the pros and cons of social media marketing? http://socialmediatoday.com/content/what-are-pros-and-cons-social-media-marketing

5.4 Customer Relationship Management

Anshari, M., Almunawar, M. N., Lim, S. A., & Al-Mudimigh, A. (2019). Customer relationship management and big data enabled: Personalization & customization of services. *Applied Computing and Informatics, 15*(2), 94–101. https://doi.org/10.1016/j.aci.2018.05.004

Gummeson, E. (2002). Rethinking marketing. In *Total relationship marketing* (2nd ed., 1–31). Butterworth-Heinemann.

Izquierdo, R. (2024, May 10). *A beginner's guide to the customer life cycle.* The Motley Fool. https://www.fool.com/the-ascent/small-business/e-commerce/articles/customer-life-cycle/

Mortati, M., Magistretti, S., Cautela, C., & Dell'Era, C. (2023, April). Data in design: How big data and thick data inform design thinking projects. *Technovation, 122.* https://doi.org/10.1016/j.technovation.2022.102688

Wining, L. (2016, February 18). *GE's big bet on data and analytics: Seeking opportunities in the Internet of Things, GE expands into industrial analytics.* MIT Sloan Management Review. https://sloanreview.mit.edu/case-study/ge-big-bet-on-data-and-analytics/

5.5 Marketing Plans

Ader, J., Boudet, J., Brodherson, M., & Robinson, K. (2021, February 21). *Why every business needs a full-funnel marketing strategy.* McKinsey & Company. https://www.mckinsey.com/capabilities/growth-marketing-and-sales/our-insights/why-every-business-needs-a-full-funnel-marketing-strategy

American Marketing Association. (2022, July 12). *The Four Ps of Marketing.* https://www.ama.org/marketing-news/the-four-ps-of-marketing/

Dahl, D. (2021, January 5). *How to write a marketing plan.* Inc. https://www.inc.com/guides/writing-marketing-plan.html

Gibson, K. (2024, February 1). *7 Marketing KPIs you should know and how to measure them.* Harvard Business School. https://online.hbs.edu/blog/post/marketing-kpis

CS5 Viral Marketing

CNN. (2023a, December 22). *Stanley x Target: All in motion collection* [image]. https://media.cnn.com/api/v1/images/stellar/prod/stanley-x-target-all-in-motion-collection-cnnu.jpg

CNN. (2023b, December 22). *Stanley x Target: Hearth and Hand by Magnolia collection* [image]. https://media.cnn.com/api/v1/images/stellar/prod/stanley-x-target-hearth-hand-magnolia-cnnu.jpg?q=w_1110,c_fill/f_webp

Issawai, D. (2022, May 17). *How the Stanley tumbler became so popular*. The New York Times. https://www.nytimes.com/2022/05/17/style/stanley-tumbler.html

Lamour, J. (2024, January 9). *The Stanley cup craze: The story behind the viral tumbler*. Today. https://www.today.com/food/trends/stanley-cup-craze-rcna132901

Vega, P., & Peltz, J. F. (2020, February 23). *How the Hydro Flask water bottle got so popular*. Los Angeles Times. https://latimes.com/business/story/2020-02-23/hydro-flask-water-bottle-why-is-it-special

Wynne, G. (2022, July 12). *The TikTok-viral drinking tumbler has been re-stocked*. Huffington Post. https://huffpost.com/entry/stanley-adventure-quencher-travel-tumbler-cup_l_629a119be4b0b1100a641396

6.0 Business Finances

SCORE Association. (2024, July 23). *Financial projections template*. https://www.score.org/resource/template/financial-projections-template

6.1 Start-Up Expenses

Amazon. (n.d.). *Standard selling fees*. Retrieved July 24, 2024 from https://sell.amazon.com/pricing

Berry-Johnson, J. (2024, April 18). *How much does a CPA or accountant cost?* Bench. https://bench.co/blog/accounting/how-much-does-a-cpa-cost

Brand, P. (2020, April 2). *Downtime in manufacturing: What's the true cost?* Oden Technologies. https://oden.io/blog/downtime-in-manufacturing-the-true-cost/

MetLife. (2022, October 18). *How much does a lawyer cost?* https://metlife.com/stories/legal/how-much-do-lawyers-cost/

Staiger, D. (2023, October 1). How to calculate square feet per employee. McCoy Rockford Commercial Interiors. https://www.mccoyrockford.com/blog/how-to-calculate-square-feet-per-employee/

SCORE Association. (2023, May). *Financial projections template* [Microsoft Excel spreadsheet]. https://score.org/sites/default/files/2023-05/SCORE%20Financial%20Projections

6.2 Payroll

McIver, E. (2022, January 27). *How long should it take your business to become profitable?* Bench. https://bench.co/blog/starting-a-business/how-long-does-it-take-business-to-be-profitable

Miranda, D., & Bottorff, C. (2022, November 24). *Part time vs. full time: Key differences you should know.* Forbes. https://forbes.com/advisor/business/part-time-vs-full-time/

SCORE Association. (2023, May). *Financial projections template* [Microsoft Excel spreadsheet]. https://score.org/sites/default/files/2023-05/SCORE%20Financial%20Projections

U.S. Department of Labor. (2024, July 1). *Consolidated minimum wage table.* https://www.dol.gov/agencies/whd/mw-consolidated

U.S. Department of Labor. (2024, March 11). Fact sheet 13: employee or independent contractor classification under the Fair Labor Standards Act (FLSA). https://www.dol.gov/agencies/whd/fact-sheets/13-flsa-employment-relationship

6.3 Sales Forecasts

AutoZone. (2022, October 21). *How long does an oil change take?* https://www.autozone.com/diy/motor-oil/how-long-does-an-oil-change-take

SCORE Association. (2023, May). *Financial projections template* [Microsoft Excel spreadsheet]. https://score.org/sites/default/files/2023-05/SCORE%20Financial%20Projections

6.4 Operating Expenses

Insureon. (2024, April 3). Small Business Insurance Costs. https://www.insureon.com/small-business-insurance/cost

SCORE Association. (2023, May). *Financial projections template* [Microsoft Excel spreadsheet]. https://score.org/sites/default/files/2023-05/SCORE%20Financial%20Projections

The Hartford. (2024, May 3). How much does small business insurance cost in 2024? https://www.thehartford.com/small-business-insurance/how-much-does-small-business-insurance-cost

6.5 Financial Analyses

Mago, M. (2020, September 28). Reporting and analyzing inventory. Harper College. https://www.harpercollege.edu/academic-support/tutoring/subjects/Chapter%206%20Review%2011th%20ed.pdf

McIver, E. (2022, January 27). *How long should it take your business to become profitable?* Bench. https://bench.co/blog/starting-a-business/how-long-does-it-take-business-to-be-profitable

SCORE Association. (2023, May). *Financial projections template* [Microsoft Excel spreadsheet]. https://score.org/sites/default/files/2023-05/SCORE%20Financial%20Projections

Index of Abbreviations

As described in *Section 1.1: A Common Vocabulary*, e-Commerce is influenced by the language (and abbreviations!) of many different industries. In an effort to keep the page count manageable, abbreviations are generally defined when introduced. Quick definitions appear below; for additional context, follow the page link.

501(c)(3)	p. 36	Not-for-profit business type defined by the U.S. Internal Revenue Code to focus on charitable work
501(c)(4)	p. 36	Not-for-profit business type defined by the U.S. Internal Revenue Code to permit political lobbying
5G	p. 8	5th Generation Broadband Cellular Network
A11y	p. 115	Accessibility in design
ABCD	p. 68	Audience, Behavior, Conditions, and Degree
ADA	p. 115	(U.S.) Americans with Disabilities Act
AI	p. 21	Artificial Intelligence
AIDA	p. 139	Attention, Interest, Desire, Action (Advertising Model)
AJAX	p. 7	Asynchronous JavaScript and XML
ANC	p. 42	Active Noise Cancellation
AR	p. 23	Augmented Reality
ARIA	p. 118	Accessible Rich Internet Application (Standards)
ASP	p. 112	Active Server Pages
B-Corp	p. 36	Benefit Corporation
B2B	p. 4	Business to Business (Transaction)

B2C	p. 4	Business to Consumer (Transaction)
B2G	p. 4	Business to Government (Transaction)
C-Corp	p. 35	Corporations subject to Corporate tax
C2C	p. 4	Consumer to Consumer (Transaction)
CAC	p. 143	Customer Acquisition Cost
CAR	p. 142	Customer Acquisition & Retention (Costs)
CDN	p. 98	Content Delivery Network
CMS	p. 115	Content Management System
COGS	p. 170	Cost of Goods Sold
CPA	p. 165	Certified Public Accountant
CPC	p. 143	Cost Per Click
CRM	p. 149	Customer Relationship Management
CSS	p. 112	Cascading Style Sheets
CV	p. 74	Curriculum Vitae (or Resume)
DBA	p. 34	Doing Business As
DDoS	p. 100	Dedicated Denial of Service (Attack)
DMCA	p. 10	(U.S.) Digital Millennium Copyright Act
DNS	p. 89	Domain Name Service
DoS	p. 81	Denial of Service (Attack)
DSA	p. 11	(EU) Digital Services Act
EDI	p. 6	Electronic Data Interchange
EU	p. 9	European Union
EULA	p. 16	End User License Agreement
FCC	p. 12	(U.S.) Federal Communications Commission
FERPA	p. 77	(U.S.) Federal Educational Rights and Privacy Act
G2G	p. 4	Government to Government (Transaction)
GDPR	p. 9	(EU) Global Data Protection Regulation
GE	p. 127	General Electric (Companies)

GUI	p. 119	Graphic User Interface
HTML	p. 112	HyperText Markup Language
ICANN	p. 93	Internet Corporation for Assigned Names and Numbers
IIS	p. 113	Internet Information Services
IoT	p. 127	Internet of Things
IP	p. 90	Internet (Communication) Protocol
ISP	p. 12	Internet Service Provider
IT	p. 130	Information Technology (Industry/Sector)
JSON	p. 6	JavaScript Object Notation
KPI	p. 154	Key Performance Indicator
LLC	p. 35	Limited Liability Corporation
LNG	p. 127	Liquefied Natural Gas
LTV	p. 143	(Consumer) LifeTime Value
MBA	p. 62	Master's (Degree) in Business Administration
MFA	p. 80	Multi-Factor Authentication
ML	p. 21	Machine Learning
P2P	p. 4	Peer to Peer (Transaction)
PHP	p. 112	Hypertext PreProcessor
R&D	p. 63	Research & Development
ROA	p. 176	Return on Assets
ROE	p. 176	Return on Equity
ROI	p. 147	Return on Investment
RoR	p. 147	Return on Relationship
S-Corp	p. 36	Small business Corporation
SBA	p. 51	(U.S.) Small Business Administration
SEO	p. 111	Search Engine Optimization
SMART	p. 68	Specific, Measurable, Achievable, Relevant, and Time-sensitive (Objective)
SQL	p. 115	(Database) Server Query Language

SSL	p. 97	Secure Socket Layer (Encryption Protocol)
SWOT	p. 67	Strengths, Weaknesses, Opportunities, and Threats
TLD	p. 91	Top-Level Domain
TLS	p. 97	Transport Layer Security
UI	p. 101	User Interface
UN	p. 141	United Nations (International Political Organization)
URL	p. 89	Uniform Resource Locator
UX	p. 101	User eXperience
VPN	p. 93	Virtual Private Network
VPS	p. 96	Virtual Private Server
VR	p. 23	Virtual Reality
W3C	p. 116	World Wide Web Consortium
WCAG	p. 116	Web Content Accessibility Guidelines
WYSIWG	p. 106	What You See Is What You Get (Editor)
XML	p. 6	eXtensible Markup Language
XR	p. 23	eXtended Reality

www.ingramcontent.com/pod-product-compliance
Lightning Source LLC
Chambersburg PA
CBHW052349220526
45465CB00003BA/1032